P9-BBQ-003

Pastor Joe's class

GOD'S WILL: YOU CAN KNOW IT

LESLIE AND BERNICE FLYNN

This book is designed for your personal reading pleasure and profit. It is also designed for group study. A leader's guide with helps and hints for teachers and visual aids (Victor Multiuse Transparency Masters) is available from your local bookstore or from the publisher.

VICTOR BOOKS

a division of SP Publications, Inc.
WHEATON ILLINOIS 60187

Offices also in Fullerton. California • Whitby. Ontario. Canada • Amersham-on-the-Hill. Bucks. England

Fourth printing, 1981

Unless otherwise noted, Scripture quotations are
from the King James Version. Other quotations are
from *The Living Bible* (LB), © Tyndale House
Publishers, Wheaton, Ill., and *The New American
Standard Bible* (NASB), © 1960, 1962, 1968, 1971,
1972, 1973, The Lockman Foundation, La Habra,
California. All quotations used by permission.

Recommended Dewey Decimal Classification: 248.4
Suggested subject headings: Will of God; Christian life

Library of Congress Catalog Card Number: 78-64361
ISBN: 0-88207-779-1

VICTOR BOOKS
A division of SP Publications, Inc.
P.O. Box 1825 • Wheaton, Illinois 60187

To our "Peggy"

Contents

Foreword
1 Does God Guide Today? 9
2 Where God's Will Can Be Found 20
3 The Inner Voice 32
4 When the Pieces Fall in Place 43
5 God Gave You a Mind—Use It 55
6 First Things First 67
7 A Step at a Time 78
8 More Circumstances:
   Ability and Advice 89
9 Delay and Pray 102
10 Fleece, Faith, and Peace 114
11 Prime Prerequisite 125
12 If I Miss God's Will 136

Foreword

A young man wonders if he should attend college. But where? And what major?

Should he marry or remain single? Fond of two young ladies, he debates which one to wed.

Will he be a missionary? If not, what line of work should he follow: architect, lawyer, mechanic?

What town should he live in? What sort of house? How many children?

If another job offer comes along, should he accept? What investments should he make? Should he enter politics?

What church should he attend? Should his children attend a secular or Christian school?

Undoubtedly, one of life's most important questions is, "What is God's will for me?" We are in need of direction for everything from "hobby to hubby."

The following pages attempt to treat more than a dozen principles of guidance gleaned from the Scriptures, and augmented by illustrations from the lives of saints of earlier decades.

Also, more than 30 present-day Christian leaders were queried as to an outstanding incident of divine guidance in their lives. Their stories illustrate these biblically valid and practical methods of guidance.

We hope that these chapters will help 20th century believers discover the will of God for their lives.

1

Does God Guide Today?

A lady received a brochure outlining a tour to Israel. She had the time, money, and strength to take the trip but wondered if it were God's will. Rereading the pamphlet just before retiring, she noted that the airplane for the trip was a 747 jet. She tossed all night, restlessly arguing the pros and cons of fulfilling a lifelong ambition to visit the Holy Land. Awaking in the morning, she looked at her digital clock. It said 7:47. She exclaimed, "It must be the Lord's will for me to take that tour."

A college sophomore thought he was in love with a brunette. He announced to everyone that it was the Lord's will for her to be his life partner. But four months later he was running around with a blonde, now loudly insisting that she was God's choice for him.

A pastor who had served as a deacon in his

9

preordination days, toyed with the idea of buying an honorary doctor of divinity from a diploma mill. Reading 1 Timothy 3:13 he was confident he had his answer, "For they that have used the office of a deacon well purchase to themselves a good degree."

George Muller, as a missionary volunteer in his early Christian experience, tried to ascertain the field to which he should go by buying a ticket on the royal lottery. What a contrast to his later experience of praying in millions of dollars to care for orphans!

Though such methods seem strange, they point up the widespread need for divine guidance. A campus worker who traveled the college circuit was asked over and over again by students, "What is the will of God for me personally?"

A Christian education leader involved in conference workshops said that whenever a seminar was devoted to finding the will of God, almost half of the conferees could be counted on to sign up for it, despite 15 other choices.

The National Sunday School Association polled attitudes of 3,000 teenagers from evangelical churches. Out of seven religious topics, "accomplishing God's will for my life" ranked first. Only 4.5 percent had no interest in the topic.

The popularity of Ann Landers and "Dear Abby," and the proliferation of counselors of all types, including computer-dating services, show that people are searching for guidance.

Nonbiblical Ways of Finding Guidance

The ancients were also concerned with discovering the will of deity. Generals, for example, wished to know when was best to attack. Pagan methods of divination included hepatoscopy (examination of the liver of sacrificial victims); observation of the flight of birds, which if to the left omened poorly (Latin word for *left* is *sinistra*); utterances of frenzied prophets like those at the oracle of Delphi; the arrangement of curiously colored and shaped stones cast on the ground; asking counsel of pieces of wood fashioned into stocks or staffs (Hosea 4:12).

Nebuchadnezzar, king of Babylon, randomly chose an arrow from his quiver, marked either "Jerusalem" or "Rabbath," to see which city he should first attack (Ezek. 21:21). Some professed to get clear guidance from the Great Pyramid of Egypt.

Sorcerers, magicians, witch doctors, palmists, fortune-tellers, and mediums have flourished in all generations. Israel was specifically forbidden to deal with the occult (Deut. 18:9-14). However, many leaders, including kings Saul and Manasseh, consulted sorcerers and were punished (1 Sam. 28:7ff; 2 Chron. 33:1-6).

The ancients used astrology to determine the divine will. Each of the planets was thought to have its particular influence on human temperament and conduct, giving us such adjectives as jovial, martial, mercurial, and saturnine. Astrology is widespread around the globe today. In the United States alone it has 10 million devotees and 40 million dabblers who are served by 10,000 full-time astrologers and 175,000 part-time practitioners. Many colleges offer courses on astrology. One of Jeane Dixon's books was subtitled "How Astrology Can Help You Find Your Place in God's Plan" in which she attempted to explain some of the godly characteristics of the apostles, through the signs of the zodiac.

To counteract astrology's wide acceptance, 186 top U.S. scientists, 18 of them Nobel Prize winners, issued a statement which appeared on the front page of the *New York Times* (9/3/75), calling astrologers "charlatans" and asserting that "there is no rational basis for the belief." The Bible warns against seeking God's plan through astrology (Jer. 10:2; Isa. 47:13-14).

Psychics flourish, especially in California. *The National Enquirer* (1/6/76) published "startling forecasts" of 10 leading seers, which did not materialize, among them: that Gerald Ford would not last out the year in the White House, that he wouldn't run for the presidency because of health, political and domestic troubles, that Nelson Rockefeller would become president in 1976, that Ronald Reagan would be the Republican nominee. So much for the psychic approach to finding God's will!

God's Guidance in Bible Times

The Lord revealed His will in many ways in Bible days. He spoke to Lot through angels, advising him to get his family out of Sodom (Gen. 19).

The Lord gave information through dreams to Abimelech (Gen. 20:3-7), to Joseph (Gen. 37:5-10), and to the wise men (Matt. 2:12).

Visions pointed the path of duty to Peter (Acts 10:9-16) and to Paul (Acts 16:9; 18:9-10).

God spoke directly to little Samuel (1 Sam. 3:6-7). Often He came in a physical appearance called a *theophany,* as to Abraham (Gen. 22:1-2), to Isaac (26:1-5), to Jacob (35:1, 9-10), and to Moses in the burning bush (Ex. 3:1-12).

God led the Israelites through the wilderness by visible phenomenon, the pillar of cloud by day, of fire by night (Ex. 40:36-38). A special star led the Magi to the Christ Child (Matt. 2:1-2, 9). Another time God gave an audible sign, the sound of marching in the tops of the mulberry trees to indicate when to attack the enemy (2 Sam. 5:24).

The casting of lots was used frequently in biblical times to select the sacrificial goat on the Day of Atonement (Lev. 16:7-10), to divide Canaan among the tribes (Num. 26:55; Josh. 18:10), and to choose a successor to Judas (Acts 1:26).

The Urim and the Thummim, placed into the breastplate of the high priest of Israel, formed the medium through which the high priest discerned the will of Jehovah in regard to important matters affecting the theocracy.

These words literally mean *light* and *perfection*, although it is unknown what the objects were. Josephus identifies them with the sardonyxes on the shoulders of the priest's ephod, and says that they were bright before a victory, or when the sacrifice was acceptable, dark when any disaster was impending.

Others think the Urim and Thummim were three stones, on one of which was written Yes, on another No, while the third was left blank. These were used as lots, and the high priest made decisions according to the reactions of these mysterious stones.

Scriptures which mention them are Exodus 28:30; Leviticus 8:8; Numbers 27:21. In Deuteronomy 33:8, Moses said to Levi, "Let thy Thummim and thy Urim be with thy Holy One whom thou didst prove. ..."

God does not usually lead in these ways today. Significantly, the last record of the lot being used was in the upper room just prior to Pentecost. Since His coming on that day, the Holy Spirit has been here to guide believers in decision-making. The opening verses of the Book of Hebrews suggest that Old Testament methods of God's communicating to man are now superceded. "God, who at sundry times and in divers manners spake in time past unto the fathers by the prophets, hath in these last days spoken unto us by His Son" (1:1-2). The Father sent the Son, then the Son sent the Spirit, who indwells every believer. In reality, all three Members of the Godhead share in helping us discover clearly the divine will.

God's Will Can Be Known

A survey taken at Chicago's O'Hare Airport asked, "Do you know God has a plan for your life?" Over 90 percent of those answering said they were not aware of this. Yet just as God led Abraham, Moses, Joshua, David, Peter, and Paul, or nearer to our time, William Carey, David Livingstone, George Müller and D. L. Moody, so today He is able to guide us.

The *possibility* of doing God's will is implied in a verse like "For whosoever shall do the will of My Father which is in heaven, the same is My brother, and sister, and mother" (Matt. 12:50). See also Matthew 7:21; John 9:31; Hebrews 10:36; and 1 John 2:17.

The Bible abounds in *promises* of God's guidance, such as "I will instruct thee and teach thee in the way which thou shall go: I will guide thee with Mine eye (Ps. 32:8). See also Psalm 48:14; Isaiah 58:11; John 8:12; and the well-known Proverbs 3:6: "In all thy ways acknowledge Him, and He shall direct thy paths."

Scripture cites people who were led by the Lord, including the Israelites through the wilderness (Ps. 136:16), David (Ps. 16:7), Paul (Acts 22:14), and supremely, Christ (John 5:30).

The Bible's *precepts* command that we "prove what is that good, and acceptable, and perfect will of God (Rom. 12:2). Paul wrote, "Wherefore be ye not unwise, but understanding what the will of the Lord is" (Eph. 5:17). James rebuked those who made plans while disregarding the will of God (4:13-15). Many times, Paul indicated he wanted to plan his schedule according to the divine will (Rom. 1:10; 15:32; 1 Cor. 4:19; 16:7).

Frequent *prayers* were made for divine light, both for the petitioner and for others. The Psalmist prayed, "Show me Thy ways, O Lord; teach me Thy paths" (Ps. 25:4). Paul prayed that the Colossians would be "filled with the knowledge of His will in all wisdom and spiritual understanding" (Col. 1:9). See also Psalm 86:11; Colossians 4:12; Hebrews 13:21.

Overwhelming evidence shows that God has a plan for His children's lives. We are not fallen leaves tossed to and fro by the autumn breeze, but children of our heavenly Father who is deeply interested in us and has a program for us. And he can communicate it to us. But how? Subsequent chapters will suggest several guidelines for discovering the will of God. For now, here are a few preliminary observations.

What God's Will Is Not

The will of God is not a treasure hunt. It's not a tantalizing package He dangles before us to tease us along, all the time encouraging us with "You're getting close."

The will of God is not to be found through some traumatic experience. God doesn't hit us over the head with His plan. Running out of gas on a Washington, D.C. street in front of the Philippine Embassy doesn't prove that a business enterprise should be started in that country. Divine leading is not found by some ingenious, haphazard method, nor by feelings, nor sensationalism, which can lead to all sorts of foolishness.

The will of God is not necessarily difficult, distasteful, or distressing. Some think God's will must be what they least want to do. Once in a while it is, but more often the opposite is true. He who plans abundant life has for us a good and acceptable and perfect will, not something odious. Often, the person who seeks God's will finds himself doing exactly what he most enjoys! God is not an ornery taskmaster, but a loving Father whose yoke is easy and whose burden is light.

The will of God is not only for religious decisions and major matters. Missionaries, pastors, and Christian workers have no corner on God's will. Doctors, teachers, plumbers, and mechanics can all find His guidance. Nor is divine direction limited to big decisions like marriage and vocation. It extends to every day of the week, and to every area of life. Little decisions made today may have important bearings on later events.

The will of God is not the same for each individual. When Peter was informed what would happen to him in old age, he asked the Lord what would befall John. Jesus told him it was no concern of his (John 21:18-22). The will of God is personal, varying with each believer.

The will of God is not a detailed blueprint, revealed in advance like a master plan. Though complete in God's mind, His will is not shown to us in its entirety, but is made known progressively, step by step. It's like an ancient scroll which you unroll from one stick to the other, enabling you to read as much of the message as you need.

The will of God is not found through an easy formula. On a stormy night at sea, a ship was trying to find a harbor. The captain, when asked how he knew when to turn the ship into the narrow entrance, replied, "See those three red lights on the shore? When they're in a straight line and become one, then I go forward!"

God has given three important lights for guidance: the Bible, the burden, and the bearings (circumstances). The Bible is from above, the burden is from the indwelling Holy Spirit, and the bearings are around us. When these three: the upper Bible, the inner burden, and the outer bearings are all in line, this may indicate we should go forward.

But lining up the lights is not always easy. Dr. Alan Redpath, for many years pastor of Moody Church, tells that when he received the invitation to come to the Chicago church, he wrestled with God's will for months. Not long before, he had written a booklet entitled, *How to Find the Will of God.* To get help for his decision he reread his booklet, and then commented, "It didn't do me one bit of good!"

No pat procedures exist for untangling the wires of guidance. Dr. O. Quentin Hyder, well-known psychiatrist of New York City, says in his book, *The People You Live With*, "When I graduated from Cambridge University, England, with my medical degree in 1955, I would have been horrified to have been told that 15 years later I would be living in New York City practicing psychiatry." He relates the steps of God's leading. After completing his internship at London Hospital, he did a one-year term of missionary work on Malta. Feeling the need of further surgical training, especially if he were to become a full-time medical missionary, he took five years of general orthopedic surgery at various hospitals in the London area, at the Royal College of Surgeons, and in Baltimore at the Johns Hopkins Hospital.

He began to feel that, though his time had not been wasted, surgery was not God's choice for him. He chose to spend a year away from medicine entirely at Fuller Seminary in California, studying the typical freshman courses. As friends prayed for definite guidance, it seemed logical to combine his medical training and spiritual concerns by becoming a psychiatrist, dedicating himself fully to the treatment of the whole man—body, mind, and spirit. Not knowing whether to remain in the West or return East, he applied to both UCLA and Columbia-Presbyterian in New York. UCLA rejected him but Columbia welcomed him. Three years later he entered psychiatric practice. For over a decade, Dr. Hyder has been counseling, lecturing, and teaching in the New York metropolitan area, and has authored two books. But the directions for his life were not laid out for him. Rather, they unfolded, a little at a time, and he proceeded accordingly.

The Master Designer, who hung the worlds in space in an orderly universe, and who created man's body with its millions of cells to work in marvelous harmony, certainly has a plan for all His children. When the Psalmist spoke of God's *ordaining* the course of the stars and of His *ordering* the steps of saints (Ps. 8:3; 37:23), he used the same Hebrew word.

Each one of us can take courage and be glad, we can say, "I belong! There is a reason for me! I'm God's child! He has a personal will for me!"

2

Where God's Will Can Be Found

A professor signed a contract in April to teach in a Christian college the following fall. In late August he received a better offer from another Christian school. He wrote the first college, "I've prayed about God's will, and I've signed with another school."

But God's will was already clear before he prayed. For the Bible teaches that when we commit ourselves to a promise, we should keep our word.

God's Revealed Will

Large areas of life are already outlined for us, with guidance that is clear, unclouded by ambiguity. In these matters we need not pray, wonder, nor waver in moral tug-of-war. We never need to seek the leading of the Lord about any subject in which the Scripture already has a command. Someone said, "It's not the things in the Bible I don't understand that bother me; it's the things I do understand!"

When Thomas Edison began an invention, he first researched everything previously written in that field. He considered that plowing cultivated ground was a waste of time. Similarly, to search elsewhere for God's will before we have studied God's plan in the Bible is futile.

A motorist would be foolish to try to find his way across country by consulting his horoscope or by casting lots at every fork in the highway instead of reading his road map. The Bible is God's guidebook. All Scripture is profitable for direction (2 Tim. 3:16-17). "Thy Word is a lamp unto my feet, and a light unto my path . . . the entrance of Thy Words giveth light" (Ps. 119:105, 130). Parallel passages equate the will of God with the Word of God (Mark 3:35; Luke 8:21). We can steer the course of life relying on the Scripture.

Misusing God's Word

The Bible was never intended to be handled in a superstitious manner. The "lucky dip" or "stop and flop" method of opening the Bible at random to find guidance is dangerous.

For example, a girl invites her fiance over for dinner which she will cook. Not knowing what to serve, she throws open the sacred Book. Her eyes fall on Numbers 11:5 with its menu suggestions of "cucumbers and the melons, and the leeks, and the onions, and the garlic."

In Tennyson's *Enoch Arden*, an incident illustrates the folly of misappropriating a verse. Because Enoch had been long gone on a sea voyage, his wife, Annie, wondered if he had been ship-wrecked and drowned, in which case she would be free to marry her would-be suitor. Unable to sleep one night, she prayed for a sign.

"Started from bed, and struck herself a light,
Then desperately seized the holy Book,
Suddenly set it wide to find a sign,
Suddenly put her finger on the text,
'Under the palm-tree.' That was nothing to her:
No meaning there: she closed the Book and slept:
When lo! Her Enoch sitting on a height,
Under a palm-tree, over him the Sun:
'He is gone,' she thought, 'he is happy, he is
     singing
Hosanna in the highest: yonder shines
The Sun of Righteousness, and these be palms
Whereof the happy people strowing cried
'Hosanna in the highest!' . . . "

Awaking, she concluded Enoch was in heaven, so she consented to marriage. But tragically, Enoch, who was not dead, came back to see his wife and her new husband together. And all this despite Annie's "guidance" from the Bible.

The classic story concerns a man in need of direction who closed his eyes, then poked his finger on a text which read, "Judas went and hanged himself." Not satisfied with that leading, he made a second stab, only to read, "Go thou and do likewise." Hoping for better results, he tried a third time, and read, "What thou doest, do quickly."

One believer, who used to open his Bible at random, found it invariably falling open at the same Psalm. While wondering why the Lord wanted him to read that particular chapter so often, he noticed the binding was broken, causing a crease that made the Bible open at that same spot.

Imagine a doctor, seeking a remedy for a patient's illness, opening his medical book at random to follow whatever instructions first meet his eye.

In Roman days, people sought guidance by taking a passage at random from the writings of Virgil. This practice was called Sortes Virgilianae (literally, casting of lots of Virgil). But believers should not be parties to this pagan practice.

Often an isolated verse from a promise box or from regular reading of the Scripture is taken out of context. A young man wishing to visit Europe one summer came across Acts 23:11, "so must thou bear witness also at Rome." He took this as guidance for a trip to Rome, whereas the statement was given to Paul under particular circumstances. Says an old ditty,

Wonderful things in the Bible I see

When they are put there by you and by me.

We must not scan Scripture to spot some detached verse, strip it from its setting, then use it as a stamp of divine approval on our formerly formed fancy. A text out of context is a pretext. Twisting and tailoring a passage misses its real meaning, can lead to delusion, wild extravagance, and impossible expectations, and cannot be called biblical guidance. Though God may choose to speak through rather a free and far-from-context fashion, it is the exception.

God Speaks through His Word
Often we are reminded of some word from the Bible which exactly suits our need. Elisabeth Elliot

tells of the day in 1956 when by a message she learned that her husband and four friends were missing in the Aucan jungle. The words of Isaiah 43:1-3 came to her almost as if they had been spoken aloud, but they were words she had memorized years before, "Fear not . . . When thou passest through the waters, I will be with thee; and through the rivers, they shall not overflow thee: when thou walkest through the fire, thou shalt not be burned; neither shall the flame kindle upon thee. For I am the Lord thy God."

When Dr. Francis Schaeffer was in the middle of preparation for his massive assignment of writing a book and narrating 10 documentary films on the rise and decline of Western culture, he wondered if he should continue, or if it was just too much. At the breakfast reading of the Bible he suddenly exclaimed to his wife, "I've just come to Ezekiel 33. It seems clear that the Lord is speaking to me. There is no turning back." He believed the lessons from that chapter, on the responsibility of a watchman to warn of the enemy, paralleled his situation, even providing the title for both book and documentary, *How Should We Then Live?* (v. 10).

Interpret the Bible Properly

The Bible differs from every other book because it was inspired by the Holy Spirit. Even though it is illuminated by the same Spirit for our understanding, the techniques for its study are much the same as for other books. Scripture is expressed in words, sentences, and paragraphs in propositional form. So we must master the precise meaning of every word, its relation to the sentence and the larger context, noticing figures of speech, dates, geography, customs and problems of the recipients, and the purpose of the author.

Since nearly half of the books of the Bible contain 10 or fewer chapters, reading a book through at one sitting is profitable. Rereading helps us outline the plan of the book, with its major segments and minor subdivisions. In our study, we first want to see what the text says, discover what it means, and then explore its application to our lives as well as to our world.

Such procedures will keep us from foolish and dangerous practices, like that of an 18-year-old who cut off his hand and was found walking along a Connecticut highway with a Bible under his arm, and bleeding heavily. Asked why he did it, he replied, "The Bible says that if your right hand offends you, you're to cut it off."

Definite Commands

One studying the Scriptures discovers hundreds of clear commands which are definitely the will of God, as well as many principles or guidelines for living.

A respected Sunday school teacher confided in a friend that she was having an extramarital affair with a married deacon, then added, "But this isn't some cheap affair you read about. This is different. You see, his wife doesn't understand him, and our love is from God!" But God had already written, "Thou shalt not commit adultery" (Ex. 20:14). The Bible makes it plain that it is wrong to cheat, steal, lie, gossip, commit fornication, murder, or covet. The moral will of God is expressed in the Ten Commandments (Rom. 2:18).

Certain basic priorities are outlined in Scripture. To follow these is to do the will of God. A sketchy overview of these guidelines includes:

Obey parents (Eph. 6:1)
Marry a Christian (1 Cor. 6:15)
Work at an occupation (1 Thes. 4:11-12)
Support your family (1 Tim. 5:8)
Give to the Lord's work and the poor (2 Cor. 8, 9; Gal. 2:10)
Rear children by God's standards (Eph. 6:4)
Meditate in the Scriptures (Ps. 1:2)
Pray (1 Thes. 5:17)
Have a joyful attitude (1 Thes. 5:16)
Assemble for worship (Heb. 10:25)
Proclaim Christ (Acts 1:8)
Set proper values (Matt. 6:19-21; Col. 3:2)
Have a spirit of gratitude (Phil. 4:6)
Display love (1 Cor. 13)
Accept people without prejudice (James 2:1-10)

When Rev. Bruce Edwards, President Carter's pastor in Plains, Georgia, took his stand to open the church to everyone, he clarified the source of his spiritual direction, "I didn't hear a voice saying, 'Bruce, take this stand.' I used the Scripture as guidance."

Many people read a chapter from Proverbs daily, thus covering the 31 chapters every month, because the book is designed to teach us "how to live—how to act in every circumstance" (see Prov. 1:2, LB).

Several New Testament commands begin with the statement, "This is the will of God" (see 1 Thes. 4:3; 5:18; 1 Peter 2:13-15). But the hundreds of pertinent commands which do not have this specific identification are just as much God's will.

Some Christians insist on the availability of a

specific verse for every decision. But the Bible does not cover every area of life. For example, television is never mentioned in Scripture. However, the Bible does have principles that could be applied to the area of questionable matters.

Principles for Doubtful Areas

Some things are always wrong, like stealing. These absolutes should never be relativized. On the other hand, Christians in various parts of the country disagree over practices like roller-skating, mixed bathing, television viewing, jewelry, short hair, long hair, and beards. Though the Bible does not contain clear "do's" and "don'ts" in these areas, it does provide principles and moral orientation to help us choose wisely. These principles reach out in three directions: selfward, manward, and Godward.

Is the practice a spiritual drag? Just as an athlete removes all heavy clothing before a mile run, the believer is given the principle to "lay aside every weight . . . and . . . run with patience the race that is set before us" (Heb. 12:1).

Is it enslaving? Even a good thing, if it controls you, is wrong, according to Paul's principle, "All things are lawful unto me, . . . but I will not be brought under the power of any" (1 Cor. 6:12). How can a conscientious believer watch TV six hours a day?

Is it harmful to the body? A scientist told a college crowd that every cigarette cuts over 14 minutes off a person's life span. Alcohol, drugs, and overeating also hurt the body and need to be overcome. The principle that applies would be, "Know ye not that your body is the temple of the Holy Ghost . . . ? For ye are bought with a price: therefore glorify God in your body" (1 Cor. 6:19-20).

Does the practice cause a weaker brother to stumble? Meat offered to idols was served at many Roman meals. A strong Christian knew that since an idol was nothing, such meat could not defile. But a weak Christian, who hadn't yet reached this state of knowledge, and who therefore had scruples about such meat, would sin if he partook. So the strong Christian was told to surrender his liberty out of love for his weaker brother, lest by partaking he influence the weaker brother to violate his conscience and thus sin. Paul stated the principle, "Wherefore, if meat make my brother to offend, I will eat no flesh while the world standeth, lest I make my brother to offend" (1 Cor. 8:13).

Though the strong has the job of educating the conscience of the weak to help him grow up spiritually, some occasions call for the strong to curtail his enjoyment and freedom.

Is it glorifying to God? An inexhaustible number of things can be done to the glory of God, but when something cannot, we should abstain. "Whether therefore ye eat, or drink, or whatsoever ye do, do all to the glory of God" (1 Cor. 10:31).

Becoming like Christ

God intends that His people be "perfect, thoroughly furnished unto all good works" (2 Tim. 3:17). God's great design is for every believer "to be conformed to the image of His Son" (Rom. 8:29). God's will is not so much geography as godliness. If we are *what* God wants us to be, then we'll probably be *where* He wants us to be.

It's not so much whether a person is to be married or unmarried, an architect or a carpenter, attend

Harvard or Wheaton, live in New York or Los Angeles, be a missionary in Africa or in India. The key to fulfilled Christian lives is becoming the persons God wants us to be. If we major in the cultivation of Christlikeness, He will lead to the course of service He had planned. God's will has more to do with our dedication than with location or vocation.

Joseph T. Bayly put it aptly, "Something is wrong when Christians are more interested in making decisions than in growth in character, in geographic placement than in holy living, in guidance than in the Guide. Our problem is not so much overemphasizing guidance as overlooking God" (Preface, *Essays on Guidance*, InterVarsity Press).

Consistently Study the Word
As Christians, we should familiarize ourselves with the Word of God, searching the Scriptures daily so that the Word will dwell in us richly (Acts 17:11; Col. 3:16; Josh. 1:8; Ps. 1:2-3).

Instead of the quick, show-me-now, lucky-dip method, the believer needs to read the Word regularly and reflectively, prayerfully asking certain questions. Is there a command here for me? A prohibition? A principle to follow? "To turn the other cheek," Matthew 5:39, is not so much a command of what to do when slapped on the face, as it is an illustration of the broader principle of nonretaliation. Is there a biblical example? We are specifically told that the idolatry, fornication, and murmurings of the Israelites in the wilderness episodes "were our examples, to the intent we should not lust after evil things, as they also lusted" (1 Cor. 10:6).

A young theologian, hearing about an uneducated cobbler well versed in the Bible, proudly thought he could ask the cobbler some questions he couldn't answer, so began, "Can you tell me what Urim and Thummin were?" The cobbler replied, "I don't know exactly, but I understand that the words apply to something that was on the breastplate of the high priest. I know that through the Urim and the Thummin the high priest was able to discern the mind of the Lord. But I find that I can get the mind of the Lord by just changing two letters. I take the Bible, and by 'usin' and 'thummin' I get the will of the Lord."

To the degree that a believer becomes acquainted with the truths of the Bible, he comprehends the will of God. With his knowledge and judgment guided by the truths of God, he will be able to "approve things that are excellent" (Phil. 1:10). A man who paid for his gas at the end of the month was given a bill that omitted one of the times his tank was filled. He rationalized, "the station will never miss it." But then the simple command, "Thou shalt not steal" flashed into his mind. He knew the will of God, and paid in full.

Paul spoke of the renewed mind, or "renewed insight" (Rom. 12:2). Spiritual insight is seeing things from Christ's point of view. The more we get into the Word, the more we will see life as God views it, and make decisions as He would have us make them.

When a matter of extreme importance came up which demanded immediate action by a committee in charge of a city-wide evangelistic crusade, the pastors on the committee were reluctant to reach any verdict in the absence of the evangelist. But the team's second-in-command told them what the evangelist would want done. When asked if he were sure he knew the evangelist's mind on the matter, he replied without the slightest hesitation, "Yes, I know this is exactly what he would do." For 20 years the second-in-command had been intimately associated with the evangelist in hours of prayer and planning. Through this closest comradeship, he had come to see through the evangelist's eyes, and to know the evangelist's mind. A close walk with the Lord through His Word will make us that sensitive to His mind and will.

In a letter written nearly 200 years ago, John Newton said, "The Word of God is not to be used as a lottery; nor is it designed to instruct by shreds and scraps, which, detached from their proper places, have no determinate import; but it is to furnish us with just principles, right apprehensions to regulate our judgments and affections, and thereby to influence and direct our conduct. Those who study the Scriptures . . . are taught to make a true estimate of everything around them, are gradually formed into a spirit of submission to the will of God, discover the nature and duties of their several situations and relations in life . . . By treasuring up the doctrines, precepts, promises, examples and exhortations of Scripture, in their minds, and daily comparing themselves with the rule by which they walk, they grow into an habitual frame of spiritual wisdom, and acquire a gracious taste, which enables them to judge right and wrong with a degree of readiness and certainty, as a musical ear judges sounds" (articles, *How God Guides in Eternity*, Nov. 1977, p. 54, taken from *Letters of John Newton* published by *Banner of Truth*).

3

The Inner Voice

Walking through the exhibition area of a large interdenominational convention, a high school senior noticed several booths promoting Christian colleges. Taking a shine to one particular school, she had an *inner feeling* this was the Lord's choice. She applied and was accepted, but lasted only one semester. Among other disappointments, the school didn't offer the major she wanted.

A college sophomore, in need of a new car, visited a used car lot. His attention was drawn toward a sporty looking job. An *inner urge* told him this car was the Lord's will. It turned out to be a lemon.

A senior in college had three boyfriends. Though she liked them all, a *hunch* seemed to say she should marry the latest fellow, about whom she knew the least. The marriage was a disaster.

Were these inner voices to blame for these three

wrong choices? In the first chapter we listed three major factors in securing guidance: the Bible from above, the burden from within, and the bearings around us. This chapter deals with the burden within.

Names for the Inner Burden

The inner burden has been given many names: inner voice, inward compulsion, sense of mission, inner compass, inside pressure, divine constraint, inner light, and a stirring within. Elijah received guidance, not from wind, earthquake, or fire, but from a still, small voice (1 Kings 19:11-18).

An Old Testament message was often called a "burden" (Isa. 13:1; 14:28; Jer. 23:33-34, 36, 38; Nah. 1:1; Hab. 1:1; Zech. 9:1; 12:1; Mal. 1:1), probably because its contents predicted judgment that weighed heavily on its hearers. Because some burdens contained no threat or denunciation, *burden* also signified a revelation, oracle, or declaration from God. A burden weighed solemnly upon the heart of the person who had to deliver it. When today we believe the Lord has something for us to do, we call it an inner burden, and say, "I feel led to do it because it's on my heart."

A Spirit-sent compunction directing a particular person to a specific task is often termed "a call." Several times Paul asserted he had been "called" to be an apostle (Rom. 1:1; 1 Cor. 1:1; Gal. 1:15). Also, many times he said he was an apostle by "the will of God" (2 Cor. 1:1; Eph. 1:1; Col. 1:1). Though Paul had a definite, objective commission to carry the Gospel to the Gentiles, his call received confirmation from the inner voice. Today, ministers and missionaries, at their ordination or commission, are expected to tell how they were called to Christian service.

The Holy Spirit Speaks Within

The genuine inner voice belongs to the Holy Spirit. Jesus was led by the Spirit into the wilderness to be tempted, and then returned "in the power of the Spirit" to Galilee (Luke 4:1, 14). It was the Spirit who led Philip to approach the Ethiopian riding in his chariot (Acts 8:29). It was the Spirit who told Peter to go with the messengers from Cornelius' house (Acts 10:19-20; 11:12). The Spirit directed Paul throughout his ministry (16:7; 20:22-23), after separating him for missionary endeavor, along with Barnabas, from the gifted leaders at Antioch (Acts 13:2). Today the Spirit still moves in the hearts of believers to grant His guidance.

How Does the Spirit Direct?

How does the Spirit guide us? Often by inward impelling. By affecting our mental processes. By putting impressions into our thinking. By energizing our minds toward some task. By stressing the urgency of some course of action. By pointing to some need. By jogging our memories. By stirring our imaginations. The compelling, insistent desire to study law, or medicine, or architecture, or the strong propensity to follow a certain course may well be the Spirit's voice within. Nehemiah wrote, "God put into mine heart to gather together the nobles, and the rulers, and the people, that they might be reckoned by genealogy" (7:5). Sometimes, the inner call is so insistent that it seems like a real voice.

Countless Christians have been directed into a

particular sphere of service by the urging of the Holy Spirit. A young man hears several missionaries, many from Africa. He begins to feel an urge, a sense of burden, a crying out of the people of that continent. He cannot evade it. He thinks much about it. After years of training, he goes as a missionary to Africa.

As a teenager listens to his pastor, he finds himself wishing he could deliver a sermon. Thoughts of preaching keep coming into his mind, till one day he realizes he is being called to the ministry. The call becomes stronger. After college and seminary come fruitful pastorates.

David Livingstone testified, "Providence seems to call me to the rigorous beyond." Dr. Robert G. Lee, famous Southern Baptist orator, relates how as a young professor he received an invitation to teach Latin at his alma mater, but "a Vesuvius, burning in my breast to preach, made me turn the offer down." Dr. Oswald Smith, missionary statesman of People's Church, Toronto, Canada, tells how as a teenager he was "fired with a desire to preach, and would lie awake nights composing sermons and preaching them over and over to himself." The renowned pastor of First Baptist, Dallas, Texas, Dr. W. A. Criswell, as a 12-year-old lad believed he would pastor a large church, and he said to himself, "In my preaching, I shall tell that life is two streams, one that leads to God, the other to the Devil. Thousands shall hear me."

Jim Vaus recounts how a remark by a Philadelphia prisoner, a walking tour of Manhattan, a cover article in *Life* Magazine on the gangs terrorizing the city, and a visit to an area known for its high crime rate, all combined to call him to work among those teenage gangs. Climactic link in his commission was a song he heard sung by a college choir, one stanza of which began, "So send I you to loneliness and longing." Vaus spent the next 16 years ministering in the slums of New York City's Spanish Harlem.

Chaplain Ray, the well-known prison evangelist, on a visit as a tourist to Sing-Sing reinforced his conviction that the Lord was calling him to a special ministry to prisoners.

Claire Killman, wife of Russell Killman, director of Haven and Home Hour, awoke one morning with a strong sense that they should drive up and spend the day with their daughter at Westmont College. It didn't make much sense as her daughter would be in classes, and her husband would lose valuable time from work. But her feeling was so strong that he agreed. Arriving at noon, they found their daughter in the dining room and spent the afternoon with her. Just before leaving, the parents learned that their daughter had been suspended for a week because of an infraction of school rules. The dean, seeing the parents on the ground, assumed they had come to drive their daughter home, when in reality the Lord, through His inner voice, had arranged for them to be there to support their daughter, as well as take her home. The daughter learned along with her parents how beautifully God works.

Is the Inner Voice always the Spirit?

In a Bible school where much emphasis was placed on guidance by the inner voice, an earnest senior girl was praying for the Lord's will after gradua- tion. "O Lord," she moaned, "show me." A couple of mischievous girls crept under her open window, intoning in solemn voice, "Come over into Spain and help us." With a yelp of praise, the girl ran through the dorm, telling her friends. "The Lord has called me to go to Spain. I heard His voice." When that evening she gave her testimony of God's leading publicly in a large church, the culprits felt that in all kindness they had to tell her the truth. She was utterly crestfallen.

Some people speak of receiving messages as if direct from God's hot line. One mother drowned her baby sobbing, "God told me to do it." People quit their jobs, drop out of school, attempt suicide, and leave their mates, all claiming, "God spoke to me."

John Wesley warned, "Do not hastily ascribe things to God. Do not easily suppose dreams, voices, impressions, visions, or revelations to be from God. They *may* be from Him, they *may* be from nature, they *may* be from the devil. Therefore, believe not every spirit, but try the spirits, whether they be from God."

Here are some tests for discerning whether the inner voice is the Holy Spirit or some impersonator, or merely the power of suggestion.

The true inner voice must be in agreement with Scripture. Some tend to think of guidance as an inward impelling by the Holy Spirit, apart from the written Word. Some even think that since they have the Holy Spirit, they no longer need the Bible. But by replacing biblical light with inward illumination, they open themselves up to all sorts of delusions. Hannah Whithall Smith, who wrote the classic, *The Christian's Secret of a Happy Life*, in another book, *Religious Fanaticism*, said, "Every fanaticism that I have ever known has begun by the following of these inward impressions . . . When people are in specially religious frames of mind, their emotional nature is always specially open to impressions, and it is certainly the most natural thing in the world for them to believe that the interior impressions which come in these solemn and sacred moments must necessarily be of the Lord" (AMS Press, New York, NY, 1976).

We must always keep in balance the two marvelous means of guidance: the Holy Bible and the Holy Spirit. The Bible is our objective authority; the Spirit our subjective. Too often, we emphasize one at the expense of the other. Stressing only the Bible leads to dry intellectualism and neglect of the influences of the Spirit. On the other hand, reliance on subjective experience grants no genuine objective guide for living. Both extremes are wrong. Since the Spirit authored Scripture, the two will never be in disagreement. Any proposed action which runs contrary to the Bible cannot be the will of God. Compulsions to cheat, steal, lie, overeat, have extramarital affairs, do not have their source in the Spirit of God, for they all run counter to the Word which the Spirit inspired. The Spirit's voice may be twofold, but His message is one. If there is a contradiction in the messages, the speaker cannot be the same.

At the transfiguration of Christ, Peter had the thrilling experience of hearing the Father's voice say, "This is My beloved Son, in whom I am well pleased" (2 Peter 1:17). Then Peter added the amazing assertion that "we have also a more sure word of prophecy" which is none other than Scripture (vv. 19-21). Catch the comparison. Though

Peter had heard God's audible voice, he said that the written word is more certain. Commenting on this thought, Charles H. Spurgeon declared that if an angel from heaven should appear to him in spectacular brilliance and announce that his name was recorded in the Lamb's Book of Life, he would confidently reply, "I am pleased that you have come in all your splendor to tell me this, but I have a higher authority that tells me I am saved. I have the Bible."

The Bible is the foundation of all guidance. The Spirit's inward promptings are not apart from the Word, but are pressures on our conscience of truths in the Word. The Spirit leads by illuminating passages and principles already given in the Scripture. George Muller said, "I seek the will of the Spirit of God through or in connection with the Word of God. They must be combined."

How important is the regular, prayerful, Spirit-led study of the Bible—otherwise we may be misled by hunches. Hannah Smith warned, "Beware of impressions, beware of emotions, beware of physical thrills, beware of voices, beware of everything, in short, that is not according to the strict Bible standard and to your own highest reason" (*Religious Fanaticism,* p. 164).

The true inner voice asks nothing irrational. Impressions from the Holy Spirit will seem reasonable to a mature Christian. They will not lead you to marry a person you have known just a week, nor suggest anything vulgar, bizarre, or eccentric.

A life-style seeking moment-by-moment direction from the inward voice of the Spirit for every routine choice, might seem superspiritual and desirable. But it would issue in confusion and comic-tragic consequences. Consider the case of the woman who each morning, having consecrated the day to the Lord immediately on waking, would then ask Him whether she was to get up, and would not move till the voice told her to dress. "Before she put on each article, she asked the Lord whether she was to put it on, and very often the Lord would tell her to put on the right shoe and leave off the other; sometimes she was to put on both stockings and no shoes; and sometimes both shoes and no stockings; it was the same with all the articles of dress . . . ." Later when seated in a room, the voice told her to get up and go out of the room, and when out, to come back. She moved from one chair to another, then was told to go stand on the front doorstep, and do all sorts of erratic things.

Hannah W. Smith tried this procedure one morning. Just as she got one spoonful of her breakfast to her mouth, the voice told her to put it back on the plate. She tried following inner impressions till near noon, when her common sense revolted. "There's no divine guidance in this at all" (pp. 184-185).

A man climbed to the top of a major bridge, precariously perching there till hundreds gathered below, because an inner voice had told him this would gather a crowd to whom he could preach the Gospel. Though we are to be instant in and out of season, Holy Spirit wisdom frees us from rash and monstrous ways by which some tactless believers barge into the lives of others.

The true inner voice will be unrelenting and persistent. Impressions fade. Emotions pass. Moods come and go, like ladies' hair styles. But the voice of the Spirit does not vacillate. Notions are here today, gone tomorrow. But the divine voice is here today, tomorrow, and six months from now. A person who responds to every conceivable appeal that comes his way, first volunteering for service in Africa, then South America, then Alaska, then seminary, then graduate school, had better wait till he receives an unshaken, continuing impression.

When little Samuel heard a voice call his name during the night, he thought it was Eli, the high priest. Not till the fourth call did Samuel know it as the Lord's voice. The Spirit's voice will persist to make Himself known with the passing of time.

Two young men, one just out of high school, the other a few years in the business world, both active in the youth group, asked their pastor how they could tell if they should enter the ministry. He replied, "Stay out—unless you can say with the Apostle Paul, 'Woe is me if I preach not the Gospel'." The high school graduate could not stay out, and has spent over 30 years in the ministry. The other young man felt no compulsion toward the ministry, but did toward business, and today holds a high position with a well-known company.

The true inner voice will find outer confirmation. A seminary student told his homiletics professor that he knew he was called to be a preacher for he had seen a cloud formation that spelled "PC," which he took as a message from God to "preach Christ." The professor who had heard him preach replied, "Those letters probably meant 'plant corn'."

The Spirit does not usually give an inner compulsion that runs counter to circumstantial evidence or the advice of capable, godly friends. If a Christian youth has a burden to become a trial lawyer, but has overwhelming speech problems, the desire is probably not of God. However, if a young lady feels an inner call to become a doctor, and it's of the Spirit, the door to medical school will open, and in good time she'll be in practice. Inner voice should be followed by outer call. It's strange to meet someone who claims to have a call to preach when no one has a call to listen.

When health considerations prevented the family of Dr. Wade T. Coggins from returning to missionary work in Colombia, South America, he had a strong impression that the Lord was leading him into some aspect of missionary endeavor in the United States. For several months the strong impression persisted, though no opportunity came along. Then one day a letter arrived from Dr. Clyde T. Taylor, then executive director of the National Association of Evangelicals, inviting Coggins to work with him in Washington. In less than a month Coggins was on the job. That was the summer of 1958. The many years of working in the Evangelical Foreign Missions Office have confirmed that inner impression of two decades ago. Today Coggins serves as Executive Director of EFMA.

An artificial distinction has been made between so-called secular and sacred work. Though we speak of "full-time" Christian service, every legitimate occupation should have a Christian dimension to it. The Reformers termed our work "vocation" or calling. No matter what job a person holds, he can devote some of his spare time to the Lord's work. But because the Spirit has the right to assign us where He chooses, every believer should be listening for that inner voice that calls each of us to our respective task, whether butcher or baker, mechanic or missionary.

4

When the Pieces Fall in Place

Before attending graduate school, Bruce Shelley and his wife had applied to a mission board for overseas service. As he was finishing his Ph.D. work at the University of Iowa, he found that their interview with the mission board's candidate committee was scheduled the same day as his oral defense of his dissertation. Later he heard that the next regular meeting of the mission board was cancelled; it would be six months before the board would meet again. Then a few days later, without seeking it, an invitation came to teach at the Conservative Baptist Seminary in Denver. Dr. Shelley, now for over 20 years a member of the faculty, comments, "This is how we got in Denver and one of the reasons we have stayed. We feel God was behind the whole thing."

God uses circumstances to guide us along the

way. Things don't just happen. Coincidence is mindless fortuity or patternless chance, whereas circumstances forge a coherent chain in the purpose of God who "worketh all things after the counsel of His own will" and "for good to them that love" Him (Eph. 1:11; Rom. 8:28).

The omniscient Lord often devises some obvious event at an opportune moment to show His will. An Egyptian caravan "happened" along just when Joseph's brothers wanted to get rid of him (Gen. 37). It just "happened" that Rebekah came to draw water when Eleazar arrived at the well (Gen. 24). It just "happened" that King Ahasuerus could not sleep one night, which resulted in his hearing a historical account which led to the rewarding of Mordecai who had uncovered an assassination attempt on his life (Es. 6).

At an uncannily right moment the phone may ring, a letter may arrive, an old friend may cross your path, or what seems an accident may happen, helping you to discern God's will.

Jim Elliot once wrote that God "pulls strings through circumstances." Circumstances may affect the direction of a believer's life in at least three ways: by confirming our path, by changing our course, or by challenging our direction.

The Confirmed Path
Paul delayed a visit to Corinth because "a great door and effectual is opened unto me" (1 Cor. 16:9). The wide open opportunity to preach the Gospel was circumstantial evidence that God wished him to stay longer at Ephesus.

For over a year Dr. Hudson Armerding, president of Wheaton College and then president of the

National Association of Evangelicals, formulated plans for an extended trip abroad, including Australia, to promote greater cooperation among evangelicals in other countries. A major problem was financing. In January 1971 a presentation of the trip to the Wheaton College Board of Trustees authorized his seven-week absence from campus, providing details could be worked out, and expenses covered. Though it seemed that the Lord was guiding, it was thought appropriate to seek some tangible sign as far as financing was concerned. March 1st was set as the deadline to cancel the plans, if such financing had not been provided by that day. On the morning of March 1st Dr. Armerding instructed his secretary to prepare letters cancelling the arrangements already made. A little later his secretary informed him that, without any hint from his office, the Alumni Association office was voting a grant toward the travel cost. Later, additional expenses were also covered, again without any solicitation of support. Circumstances confirmed the will of God in the undertaking of this trip. "When He putteth forth His own sheep, He goeth before them" (John 10:4).

Years before, circumstances had also played an important part in Armerding's career. Already approved as missionaries under the China Inland Mission, he and his wife were prevented from going to China. Then a student at Harvard University taking Chinese, Armerding was approached by the president of Gordon College to teach there, but replied he thought he was called to missionary service.

He shared his dilemma with a veteran missionary who asked what opportunities were open. Armerding told him the only opportunity was to teach at Gordon. The missionary said he should accept this offer.

When Armerding protested, saying he was called to be a missionary, the veteran assured him that if he would take the opportunity that was open, he would be doing the will of God, since He circumstantially orders our affairs. Armerding took the Gordon position.

A pastor, burdened to start a Christian children's home, was stopped on his way home from church one night by a policeman who told him of three small, hungry boys who had been abandoned by their mother in a shack at the edge of town. The policeman knew nothing of the pastor's vision. Unable to sleep well, the pastor rose early, found the boys and brought them into his own home. A few days later he was offered an unfurnished house for $10 a month, and the children's home was launched.

Circumstances played a part in a romance reported in a *Power Magazine* article, "A Modern Love Story." When an Asbury College quartet sang in an Illinois church for a two-week campaign, a girl in the church and a member of the quartet, Ruth and John, became enamored of each other. Their whirlwind courtship was to be subjected to a year's separation when the quartet was on a round-the-world trip. If still in love at the end of the year, they would become formally engaged.

In earlier years John had dedicated himself to missionary service in India where he had grown up with his missionary parents. But through the years the call had grown dim, as music seemed to capture his interest. On the tour he again dedicated himself to be a missionary in India but wondered about Ruth's reaction, for he had not mentioned his missionary background to her.

Facing the possibility that he might lose her, he wrote the hardest letter of his life. He told her that God had called him to India, and that if she had no desire to go there, they could be no more than friends. John knew it would take a month for her to get his letter, and another month for her reply to reach him.

A month later, about the time his letter was reaching America, a letter came from Ruth. She wrote how one evening at prayer meeting she had read a folder written by John's father in India. "While reading about the great need in India, the Spirit asked me if I would be willing to go there if John were called. I'm just writing to tell you that if God ever calls you to India, I will be willing and glad to go with you."

Their letters had crossed as the Spirit had been dealing with each of them. Both took this as circumstantial evidence that God meant them for each other. In 1941 they sailed for missionary service in India where they spent many terms of service. Today John and Ruth Seamands serve at Asbury Seminary where he is Professor of Christian Missions.

The Changed Course

Sometimes circumstances beyond our control alter the course of our lives. Joseph left his father's house to seek his brothers who sold him as a slave to Egyptian traders. However he felt about it then, later he could tell his brothers that God used the episode to save many lives (Gen. 50:20).

When the Israelites escaped Egypt, the Lord led

them a roundabout way through the wilderness, for the direct route would have brought confrontation with the Philistines. The resultant war would probably have made them return to Egypt (Ex. 13:17-18). God's detours make the long way turn out to be the shorter way after all.

What may seem like an accident may turn out to be an incident in the divine plan. Our disappointments may be His appointments. The ragings of Saul of Tarsus scattered the saints of Jerusalem throughout Judea and Samaria, forcing them to preach the Word out beyond the holy city (Acts 8:4).

Opposition forced Paul to leave Thessalonica and Berea, to preach the Gospel elsewhere (Acts 17:10, 14). The two-hour uproar in the Ephesus amphitheatre indicated to Paul it was time to visit the churches of Macedonia (20:1). Though Paul came to Rome under circumstances he never chose, he accepted them as divinely ordered for the furtherance of the Gospel (Acts 28:30-31; Phil. 1:12-20).

Trouble is not necessarily an indicator of being out of God's will. Job's ordeal didn't signify he was out of God's path. Jesus told His disciples to sail across the sea of Galilee, knowing their boat would meet a strong storm. Jesus Christ, who followed the divine will perfectly, suffered conflict with family, townsfolk, and national leaders.

C. Stacey Woods, one of the pioneers of Inter-Varsity, relates that when he received an invitation in 1934 to become InterVarsity Christian Fellowship General Secretary to Canada, he declined. He had no particular interest for work among university students, especially in a cold climate. Also, his plans were already formulated, for he had a ticket

to India to work among English-speaking school-
boys for two or three years before proceeding to
Australia to be ordained in the Church of England.
Convicted that he had acted too quickly without
seeking the Lord's will, he asked God's forgiveness.
Within three days three things happened. He received letters from his father and mother, question-
ing his proposed journey to India, suggesting it
might be motivated by a desire to travel. Then
came a cable from the missionary in India cancelling his proposed trip because of his sudden re-
call to England. The next morning a second letter
came from the Canadian IVCF, still convinced he
was God's man for their job. Woods accepted the
job provisionally for one year. He concluded his
work as General Secretary in the fall of 1952 (*Some
Ways of God,* InterVarsity Press, p. 44-45).

Some detours in life are forced upon us, but
others come by "chance" circumstances. Wendell
P. Loveless, who directed Moody Bible Institute's
radio station in its early years, got into radio by
"accident." Formerly a successful sales manager, his
first job at Moody was writing letters. Representing
the Institute at an exposition where he gave away
tracts, he drew a crowd with a student cornet trio.
When a radio station booth across the aisle couldn't
get prospects to sample its wares, it invited Moody's
trio over, and were so pleased they offered Moody
free time on Sunday. Drafted for the first broadcast, Loveless did so well he was asked to serve as
director of Moody's own station started soon after.
Loveless twice refused the job for he saw no future
in radio. Under his leadership the station grew to a
place of major influence in the Midwest.

Interruptions of our plans, either minor or drastic,

may be regarded as God's rearrangement of His will for us.

The Challenged Direction

Adoniram Judson headed for India, expecting to be a missionary there, but when he arrived, he was not permitted to land. So he disembarked at the next port where the ship docked, Rangoon, Burma, in which country he spent his life in a remarkable pioneer missionary work.

Judson's experience was like that of Paul, who when he tried to enter Bithynia, "the Spirit suffered them not" (Acts 16:7). With that door closed he took the open door westward to Troas, there receiving the vision of the Macedonian man asking for help (vv. 8-9).

When a door opens and other factors of guidance agree, it's probably God's will. If the door closes firmly, thank God, back up and wait. God's closing of a door does not show lack of leading. That *is* His leading. We don't need to feel unspiritual if people ask what happened to our plan. We merely tell them the Lord closed the door on us, just as He did on Paul.

Often a closed door means God has something better for us. Robert C. McQuilkin volunteered for overseas missionary service after a message by the father of martyred Betty Stam. On Thanksgiving Day he picked up the evening paper to read that the boat on which they were scheduled to sail had caugh fire and sunk in New York Harbor. The next boat would sail in three months and refused to take children. Robert and his wife prayed that if the Lord did not want them to go, the mission would change its orders for them. Shortly after, a cable came from the field, "Do not have McQuilkins come; keep them on home deputation." Later McQuilkin became president of Columbia Bible College, and a forceful missionary statesman.

Suzanne Johnson, former Miss Illinois and well-known Gospel singer, developed her talent in opera, and eventually performed in *Carmen* with the Cincinnati Opera. Contemplating more training in Europe, she saw God step in and stop her budding operatic career. After 11 years of marriage, she was pregnant. In the months of confinement the Lord showed her she had been trying to serve two masters. The closed door led her to rededicate her life to Christ.

Closed Doors Can Be Opened

A closed door does not necessarily point to God's will. Perhaps the door is neither tightly shut nor locked, and would yield to a little push or gentle knock. The parents of Moses did some pushing in the face of the death decree for all baby boys, and saved their son (Ex. 2:1-10). Nehemiah, burdened to see the walls of Jerusalem rebuilt, faced several closed doors, but he opened them all (Neh. 6:15). The four men carrying the palsied victim to Jesus, and finding the doorway blocked with people, did not conclude it was therefore not God's will for them to get in. Instead they climbed on the roof and broke a hole large enough to let the palsied down in front of Jesus, who seeing their faith healed the victim (Mark 2:4).

A pastor, who for several years had received free time from the local radio station for a daily morning devotional program, was given notice that the program was to be dropped. The pastor countered by asking if he could ask for an expression from the listeners as to their wishes. The mail response was so overwhelming that the station manager asked the pastor to continue the broadcast.

A Warning about Circumstances

Some people tend to make circumstances 95 percent of their guidance. But overemphasis on circumstances can be dangerous. Just as a closed door does not always indicate God's will, neither does an open door always confirm divine guidance.

When King Saul was pursuing David and learned he was nearby, he wrongly concluded it was God's will for him to kill David (1 Sam. 23:7).

Later when David came on sleeping Saul, David's general suggested that God had delivered the enemy into David's hand to kill, but David refused to let this set of circumstances dictate the murder of Saul (1 Sam. 26:7-9).

When disobedient Jonah found at Joppa a ship going to Tarshish, he might have concluded that God wanted him to go westward instead of east to Nineveh, especially since there happened to be space on board, and he had money for the fare. When a child of God wishes to avoid the will of God, Satan often has a way of making circumstances favorable (Jonah 1:3).

Decisions should not be based on clever coincidences. To dream of an airplane, then to wake up to a phone call from an old friend in California, does not indicate God's leading for a trip west. Someone called this the "simultaneous experience" approach. If a fellow gets a letter from a girl, right after praying for a mate, this does not mean she is God's choice. When a married woman was thrown together with another woman's husband on a church committee, requiring late meetings and frequent driving home together, they concluded wrongly that being thrown together alone so often indicated God's will was for them to have an affair. Although circumstances can affirm God's will, they should not be relied on totally—especially if the end result is contrary to biblical principles.

Check Circumstances Against Other Criteria

Circumstances should always be tested against the Word of God. Any availability of a boat going westward should have been cancelled out in Jonah's thinking by God's previous command to go to Nineveh.

Apart from the Bible, circumstantial evidence can be misread. "It's a double highway, no traffic, and the middle of the night, so why not go 70 miles an hour?" But what about verses that command obedience to the laws of the land? (Rom. 13:1; 1 Peter 2:13)

Keep in mind the three major methods of finding the will of God repeated in previous chapters: the Bible above, the burden within, and the bearings without. Or to restate: the divine command, the inner call, and the outer circumstances. According to the late president of Wheaton College, Dr. V. Raymond Edman, these three lines of evidence helped lead the Wise Men to Bethlehem. He suggested the Magi may have had Scripture ("There shall come a Star out of Jacob"—Num. 24:17), a stirring in the heart, and a star, circumstantially adapted to their limited knowledge of the heavens.

The same three lines converged to convince Peter to preach in Gentile Cornelius' home. Peter had heard the Great Commission, which ordered the Gospel preached to all nations. Then after the vision which taught that no one was unclean in God's eyes, he had the Spirit's call to accompany the three men who were seeking him. And finally, at that moment the three men came knocking at his door (Acts 10:9-20). So, verse, voice, and event all united to guide Peter to preach to Gentiles.

George Muller said, "I take into account providential circumstances. These often plainly indicate God's will in connection with His Word and Spirit."

However, since circumstances may be so easily misunderstood, they should carry the least weight. The Word and the Spirit are the prime pointers of God's leading. But usually circumstances ultimately fall in place, like the last piece of a jigsaw puzzle as a comforting supporting corroborative evidence in finding God's will.

F. B. Meyer, saintly English preacher, said, "When we want to know God's will, there are three things which always concur: the inward impulse, the Word of God, and the trend of circumstances. Never act until these three things agree."

5

God Gave You a Mind—Use It

Dawson Trotman, founder of the Navigators, used to say, "The Lord gave you a lot of leading when He gave you a brain." Though some of our choices may require supernatural direction, God expects us to use our own brain power and thought processes. Our intellects, though not infallible, can reason out many problems of guidance through logic or common sense.

Made in God's image, we have the ability to reason, weigh facts, analyze, and make intelligent decisions. To shove our minds into neutral while we seek guidance through hunches or impressions is to deny our God-given humanity.

God saves our heads as well as our hearts, so that we can use our "thinking caps" in discerning His will. Jesus told us to love God with all our mind (Matt. 22:37).

55

Use Your Mind to Find God's Will

As we seek illumination from the Lord, we need to also engage in disciplined study of the Scriptures, for they tell us many things about using our minds. For instance, right after a promise of guidance, we are told not to be "as the horse, or as the mule, which have no understanding" (Ps. 32:9).

Joseph used reason in choosing Goshen for his brothers to settle in, for it suited their shepherd occupation, was somewhat isolated from the Egyptians, provided protection for population expansion, and was closer to Canaan (Gen. 46:31-34).

Though Moses had firm promises of divine direction by means of the cloud and fire for the wilderness journeys, he asked his in-law, Hobab, to come with them, because of his knowledge of the difficult mountainous terrain ahead (Num. 10:31). Though Hobab refused, the episode shows the willingness of Moses to use human judgment for securing guidance.

When the Lord offered David a choice among three punishments for his sin of numbering the people, David used his judgment to choose pestilence, for in the choices of famine and war, he would fall into the hands of human agents who could be cruel or unjust (2 Sam. 24:10-15).

When the problem of the neglected widows arose in the early church, the apostles said, "It is not reason that we should leave the Word of God, and serve tables" (Acts 6:2). Good thinking called for the selection of deacons to handle the table-serving, thus freeing the apostles for their proper ministries.

How often in matters requiring the Lord's leading, we read words like, "Have ye not read?"; "Let every man be fully persuaded in his own mind";

"I speak as to wise (sensible) men"; "judge ye what I say" (Matt. 19:4; Rom. 14:5; 1 Cor. 10:15). When Barnabas found the work of Antioch too taxing for one man, his mental processes led him to seek the help of a capable assistant, Saul of Tarsus (Acts 11:22-26).

Jesus Used His Mind

The Lord didn't flip a coin or put out a fleece to determine the Father's will. When He saw the crowds, He reasoned He should begin teaching (Matt. 5:1-2). When He saw the sick, He concluded He should heal them. When His enemies wanted to kill Him, logic told Him to leave the area (Matt. 12:14-15). He chided the Pharisees for not using judgment concerning the signs of the times, while using it to determine the weather (Matt. 16:1-3).

He underscored the importance of computing the cost before building a tower or going to war (Luke 14:28-32). Jesus commended the unjust steward for his prudent foresight, though not for his unprincipled conduct (Luke 16:1-9). Jesus condemned the servant for not having enough sense to put his master's money out for interest, and instead burying it in the ground (Matt. 25:24-27).

Jesus did not encourage seeking some divine flash of lightning or any other gimmick for guidance. He refused to bypass the use of His mind, but exercised sound judgment in making decisions (Luke 4:42-44; John 6:15).

Paul Used His Mind

When Paul received the vision of the man of Macedonia, he made a beeline for that province. But where in Macedonia? Why not the chief city—

Philippi? But where in Philippi? Paul knew that Jews often met by a river, especially when the group had too few men to organize a synagogue. Paul's judgment was correct. Before long a strong church was established at Philippi (Acts 16:7-13).

Learning of a plot on his life when about to embark on a boat to Syria, Paul changed his plan and returned overland (Acts 20:3). Paul's manner of making decisions, though subject to the will of God, evidenced the use of reason. Paul never threw his mind overboard.

Old-fashioned, Common Sense

Some things we need not pray over, simply because common sense dictates the answer. A Greek word which means "sound-minded" appears in one form or another several times in the New Testament. Sensibility, soberness, discretion, or sound judgment is to be a trait of Christians and especially of church leaders (Titus 2:2, 5-6; 1 Tim. 3:2). Paul said to think soberly (Rom. 12:3). Peter told believers to live soberly (1 Peter 4:7).

Common sense is that practical truth about life that is useful in conducting our daily affairs. Common sense warns us we may get in trouble if we break the law. If we play with matches, we may start a fire. If we become overweight, we make ourselves candidates for heart trouble. If we don't get our sleep, we won't be our keenest. If we smoke, we may get lung cancer. If we overwork, even in Christian work, we may lower our resistance. If we wait till the night before a paper is due to prepare it, we may not do our best. To drive while intoxicated is foolhardy.

Common sense suggests: that before buying a

second-hand car we have a good mechanic go over it; that money be invested wisely; that buying quality is preferable to cheap material that will wear out four times sooner; that broaching a touchy topic is unwise when your mate is not feeling well.

Elisabeth Elliot told the 16,000 young people at the triennial Urbana '76 convention, "To do God's will . . . means going to bed at a sensible hour, grooming yourself carefully, watching your weight, cutting out the junk food."

Though God's will covers every area of life, the Lord does not give verse or voice for every minor decision we must make, but directs through our common sense. We do not choose winter dress in summer, nor an evening gown for a swimming party. It's not necessary to agonize for divine leading over every choice between vanilla or strawberry ice cream, a blue or red tie, or beef or lamb. His will leaves such choices to our judgment or preference.

When faced with choice of college, ask several pertinent questions: Is it accredited? Does it offer my major? Can I afford it? Can I live close to the main buildings, or will I have a half-mile walk? Visit the campus. Listen to some teachers. Does it have an InterVarsity or Campus Crusade group? Is there a good church nearby?

When faced with a job offer in another city, a breadwinner must ask some common sense questions: What about the cost of living there? Housing? Taxes? Good schools? Will uprooting from friends have a harmful effect on mate and children? Is there a Bible-teaching church with a good program for young people? Does the overall pattern make good sense?

A young lady awoke at 2 A.M. with the impression

that she should marry a young man whom she had dated just three times. She accepted the suggestion as divine guidance. The marriage did not survive. Common sense would require a longer courtship, giving opportunity to learn each other's characteristics, strengths, and weaknesses. Each should ponder, "Are we suited? Enjoy the same things? Get embarrassed at the other's manners? Have similar ideas about money?"

When Moses' father-in-law found the great leader of the Israelites spending from morning to night judging every case himself, common sense told him that Moses would ultimately wear himself out; so he suggested the appointment of subordinate judges over smaller groups (Ex. 18:13-17).

"A prudent man forseeth the evil, and hideth himself" (Prov. 22:3). A car owner in the North will put snow tires on his car before winter arrives. A pretty, young, new convert kept asking a handsome Christian young man to teach her the Bible alone in out-of-the-way locations. Common sense warned him that he was placing himself in a compromising position.

The temptation to Jesus to jump off the temple pinnacle was against all common sense, and was tempting God. Sometimes the line between faith and presumption is difficult to discern. A missionary appointee, moved by need of the inner city, gave away much of the money saved for mission equipment, confident God would send more money to supply his need. On the field he was so hampered by lack of equipment that he had to return home to raise more support.

We should not do that which seems illogical or unsound, and claim that, because it's odd, God is leading us. A doctor, called to the home of a terminal patient, was about to give sedation for her intense pain. As the doctor prepared the hypo, a young neighbor, a new and overenthusiastic believer, exclaimed, "Can't you see I'm going to pray? Wait till I'm through." Though the doctor suggested he administer the hypo as the prayer was offered, the youth insisted the doctor stop everything till the prayer was finished. For 10 awful minutes the doctor sat with folded hands while the youth prayed and the patient writhed in agony. The doctor's common sense told him he should have alleviated the pain immediately.

If you come to a fork in the road where routes are clearly numbered, you don't pray about which highway to take; you examine the map. In the average situations that confront us, the Lord expects us to consult our minds. One household had a favorite expression, "Put it through the think machine." Often, a little reasoning goes a long, long way.

Think Things Through

Experts in the field of decision-making list these steps in the process: identify the problem, determine the alternatives, and compare the alternatives. Then select the most appropriate.

How does a missionary society decide to enter a new field? Though the decision may never be an easy one, among the definite steps always taken is the intellectual exercise of research. When research revealed that eastern Mindanao was the fastest growing region in the Philippines, that only 2.1 percent of the people were members of evangelical churches, that the people were responsive to the

Gospel, an evangelical missionary society decided to work there.

Robert Dugan, a Baptist pastor for 18 years, resigned his Colorado church to run for U.S. Congress. When people would occasionally ask, "What's a nice pastor like you doing in politics?" he would answer in the Lord's words, "As My Father has sent Me into the world, so send I you." He says, "I evaluated the possible directions my life could go, searched biblical principles like the one quoted above, and decided to resign my pastorate to run for Congress. Many Christians cannot bring themselves to say, 'I decided,' but I'm convinced that's where the responsibility lies. If I am in a position where I honestly want to glorify the Lord with my life, I don't seek a mystical experience; I don't major in subjective feelings; I obviously pray and ask God to guide the intellect and will that He has given me, believing that in such a situation He will guide the 'sound mind' He has promised."

Bill Bright of Campus Crusade terms his method of ascertaining God's will the "sound-mind" principle.

To live in the will of God requires that we determine our goals, decide those that have priority, analyze the best way to reach them, and then start working those plans which lead to our goals. All these activities certainly require thinking.

Hard figuring about priorites will enable multi-gifted Christians to avoid the danger of overcommitment to too many worthy projects and of too little time for family, friends and fun. Guidance by the Spirit does not mean ignoring our God-given intellects and common sense. Rather, we should gather all the available data, and then try to make the most sensible decision. The late Paul Little said, "God cannot guide you on the basis of facts you do not know."

A Balance Sheet

A frequent practice in decision-making is the use of a balance sheet. George Muller, as a regular part of his procedure in ascertaining the will of God, would take a sheet of paper, draw a line down the center. On one side he would list the facts favoring the proposition; on the other, the opposing points. He would prayerfully meditate on this balance sheet several days, adding pros and cons as they came to mind. Sooner or later he reached a conclusion as to which course to follow. Muller testified that never once did he find this balance sheet method to be in error.

When John Wesley fell in love with Grace Murray, a widow and Methodist class teacher, he weighed the pros and cons of marriage in his logical mind. He rated her potential role in seven areas: housekeeper, nurse, companion, friend, fellow-laborer in the Gospel, her gifts, and the fruits of her labors. His analysis indicated he should marry her. Unfortunately his brother Charles, convinced that marriage would curtail John's ministry, galloped over to Grace Murray's home where his emotional outburst led her to a hasty marriage with another man.

Dr. Alan Redpath, former pastor of Moody Church in Chicago, as a youth faced the serious issue of whether the Lord was calling him out of business as a chartered accountant on the staff of Imperial Chemical Industries, Ltd., into the ministry. Advised against the ministry by his friends, and untrained, Redpath took a piece of paper and drew a line down the middle. On one side he put "arguments in favor of staying in business," and on the other, "arguments in favor of going into the ministry." He wrote down as many reasons as he could think of under each heading. They numbered the same when he began. But after a year of prayer and Bible study with the pros and cons in mind, every argument in favor of staying in business had been wiped out.

When prisoner Paul had to decide whether he would go back from Caesarea to Jerusalem for trial, or appeal to Caesar and be tried at Rome, he must have listed the pros and cons, at least mentally. The arguments weighed heavily on the side of appealing to Rome. Perhaps he reasoned, "If I go back to Jerusalem, an attempt will likely be made on my life, and my trial may not be fair. Why not ask for Rome, for my work was done at Jerusalem when I delivered the offering for their poor. Besides, the Lord told me I would witness at Rome. Here's my chance for a free, government-paid trip, and though it will be awesome to stand before Nero, Rome is noted for its fairness, which could mean release for more missionary endeavor." Logic dictated Rome (Acts 25:1-11) and so to Rome Paul went.

A suggested refinement of the balance sheet methodology is to assign points to each pro and con, according to importance. Three points can be penciled in beside each reason of major import, two for a factor of moderate significance, and one for an argument of minor import. When the figures are totaled, often the evidence is overpoweringly decisive.

Human Reason is Limited

Though we have stressed the mind in the decision-making process, we must utter a caution. Common sense falls short of omniscience. When told by the Lord to let his net down for a catch, Peter's reasoned conclusion after years of experience was, "We've toiled all night and caught nothing. There's nothing there now." But when he grudgingly lowered the net, the mammoth catch proved the error of his expert judgment (Luke 5:4-7).

Because the mind was darkened at the Fall, man cannot by wisdom know God, nor necessarily find His will. The tainted intellect thinks with bias, rationalizes motives, and fails to see hidden selfishness and self-interest. "There is a way that seemeth right unto man, but the end thereof are the ways of death" (Prov. 16:25). "Let not the wise man glory in his wisdom" (Jer. 9:23).

This is why the Book of Proverbs warns, "Lean not unto thine own understanding" (3:5). This verse doesn't mean that we are to stultify our minds, but rather that, as we employ our intelligence to the best of our ability, we recognize its fallibility and seek the enlightenment of the Holy Spirit.

Sometimes the Spirit may lead a Christian to make a decision contrary to reason, like the student who stuttered but felt called to be a trial lawyer. Despite his handicap and vehement opposition of family and friends, he entered law school, marvelously overcame his speech irregularity, and enjoyed years of effective courtroom practice. God's thoughts, higher than finite intellects, may sometimes seem curious, but usually they will harmonize with reason.

In the previous chapters we looked at the three

major methods of finding the will of God: the Bible from above, the burden from within, the bearings from without. Some add a fourth, the use of reason, or common sense. Our thinking faculty is needed in applying the truths of Scripture to daily living. Our critical faculty is essential in distinguishing between an irresponsible inner urge and a true burden of the Spirit. And our reasoning is indispensable in assessing the outer bearings of circumstances.

Paul urged, "Wherefore be ye not unwise, but understanding what the will of the Lord is" (Eph. 5:17). A free rendering might be, "Don't be stupid, but figure out the will of God." The verb *understand* has the idea of *bringing together*, sorting out the facts, synthesizing them to reach a sound conclusion. In verse 18, Paul explained where help may be found for solving our problems, in the filling of the Spirit. "Be filled with the knowledge of His will in all wisdom and spiritual understanding" (Col. 1:9).

6

First Things First

Dr. V. Raymond Edman, former president of Wheaton College, relates how as a college student he had an opportunity to travel to South America with a classmate. Excitedly, he told his plans to a professor, who without enthusiasm asked, "Doesn't that mean that you will leave school before commencement?" When Edman answered "yes," the unimpressed prof continued, "I question that this is the Lord's will for you. I believe we always should wait for the corner. When you signed up for the school year, you agreed to be at school until commencement. That means that commencement day is the 'corner' when the Lord's will will take another turn for you. When we do not wait for the corner, it is too easy to willfully step out of the Lord's will."

After pondering these words, Edman changed

his plans, rejected the enticing opportunity, and on commencement day the Lord opened another door that proved more wonderful.

Do That Which Is Now and Near

True guidance is never contrary to plain duty. Normally, God's will is the job at hand. One man testified that the best advice he ever received was, "Do the next thing." He said this procedure was especially helpful when he didn't know God's will in a situation.

You ask: "What's the will of God?"
Well, here's the answer true:
"The nearest thing, that should be done,
That He can do—through you!"

—E. C. Baird

It's not so much what God wants me to do way off in the distant future. But what does He want me to do today? The Christian life is a day-by-day proposition. Manna sufficient for one day greeted the Israelites each morning. We pray for our daily bread. The Bereans searched the Scriptures daily. We are to take up our cross daily. Similarly, we should do the Lord's will day by day.

Dreamily longing for God's far-off will can be a real enemy unless we do God's will today. The brilliance of tomorrow's sun can blind us to the duty of today. A believer from Africa reported to a North American church about the spread of the Gospel on his continent. A member of the congregation approached him, "I've been thinking that perhaps I should serve the Lord in Africa myself."

The African asked, "What are you doing to serve the Lord here in your country?"

"Not much of anything," came the reply.

"Then, please," countered the African, "don't go to Africa to do it."

Bishop Taylor Smith, Chaplain-in-chief of British forces during World War I, kept this motto on his desk, "As now, so then." Doing God's will today will help us discover it tomorrow. A succession of days doing God's will means a life of walking His divinely ordered path. God's will is that which is now, near, and next.

God's Will May Be Humdrum

The will of God may be the undramatic and often monotonous repetition of daily tasks. A daughter whose duty was to do the dishes after the evening meal would not be doing the Lord's will by dilly-dallying around awhile, then running off to youth Bible study, and neglecting the assigned job.

God's will is first things first. For the student it's that assignment. For the office worker, it may be tedious clerical work. For a mechanic, doing a good repair job on the next car. For the housewife, getting meals, doing housework, and taking care of the children. For all of us, it's throwing the covers off and getting our feet on the floor, when the alarm goes off.

When her first baby came along, Mrs. Lillian Graffam, wife of Dr. Everett S. Graffam, many years the Executive Director of World Relief Commission, says she felt like a "nothing" because she had to give up her deep involvement in church activities. "I had a gnawing feeling that now I couldn't work for the Lord. Just being a housewife and mother didn't appear to be very useful in the Lord's service. I asked the Lord to show me His will. In seven words God showed me that the only difference was location, not association, 'For we are laborers together with God' (1 Cor. 3:9). I no longer felt like a 'nothing.' Through the years this knowledge sanctified the drudgery that is part of housekeeping and mothering. I learned the art of intercession while ironing shirts. He revealed Himself in the commonplace over and over."

One lady did so many kind deeds for other families in need that she neglected her own husband and children. But the Bible dictates that, like charity, the will of God begins at home. Interestingly, Paul links understanding the will of God with the duties of husbands, wives, parents, children, employers and employees (Eph. 5:17; 6:9). God's will means a daily job well done, even though in an unglamorous spot. In C. S. Lewis' *Screwtape Letters*, one of Satan's great strategies is to encourage postponement of known duties.

On the other hand, God's will certainly includes the enjoyment of present pleasures: the aroma of a flower, the taste of fine food, the music of a symphony, the hues of a sunset, the company of a friend. We miss God's design when we fail to savor the joys of the moment. Jim Elliot said, "Live to the hilt every situation you know is God's will."

On occasion an emergency will take precedence over regular routine. The priest and Levite should have put schedule aside to help the wounded Jew. If an accident occurs outside a home, God's will for the housewife will be to drop her preparation of the evening meal and be a Good Samaritan. She could perhaps phone the police, run outside to comfort the injured, invite the unhurt, upset folks inside for coffee while waiting for police.

By sitting at Jesus' feet, Mary chose God's will, while Martha should have been content to serve a less elaborate meal, so as to devote more time listening to the Master. Hannah Whithall Smith said, "My guidance mostly came in very commonplace ways, and chiefly through impulses of kindness and courtesy. Nearly always when I did things to be kind to them (people), without any especial thought of guidance, they were very apt to turn out to have been the most direct guidance possible" (*Religious Fanaticism*, p. 251).

Should We Change Jobs When Converted?

Does God normally expect people to give up their jobs upon conversion? The New Testament speaks definitely to the question. Three times within a few short verses Paul tells new believers to remain in the same job which they had at conversion. "Let every man abide in the same calling wherein he was called" (1 Cor. 7:20, see also vv. 17, 24). A mechanic, when saved, should remain in the same profession.

This doesn't mean that a person cannot change jobs. Nor does it mean that he won't be called into the Lord's work, requiring surrender of occupation to get schooling to train for his new sphere of service. But if in the first flush of conversion a mechanic feels a hankering to leave the job and become a full-time Christian worker, he should be slow to make any change. D. L. Moody warned in the Boston Tabernacle that converts should not give up their business or daily job to go full-time in the Lord's work. They were to wait till God called and sent.

When God wanted a missionary job done in Asia

and Europe, He did not choose everybody in the church at Antioch, but just two key leaders, to be later joined by a few others from other churches. No huge exodus from every church was intended by the Lord. Believers were challenged to self-denial, sacrifice, and suffering. But that all should leave everyday jobs to become traveling missionaries never crossed their minds.

A layman in his occupation is as much in the will of God as a missionary or preacher. It is God who decides where His laborers work. God does not so much place man in a new location as He creates a new man in his present location. Transportation does not a missionary make. Neither does failure to cross the ocean prevent a man from being a missionary, for a man can witness right in his place of employment.

To some will come the pressing, persistent pushing of the Holy Spirit to move into full-time work. The *Bethel Seminarian* (St. Paul, Minn.) devoted part of its January 1977 issue to the matter of a mid-career shift into the ministry. It contained the testimony of a policeman who at age 35 entered Bethel Seminary and was led into pastoral ministry. Dean Gordon Johnson wrote that such decisions should not be made without careful and prayerful consideration of all the implications involved. Seek advice from church and denominational leaders, seminary personnel, and others who have made similar decisions. Involve wife and children in the decision-making process because sacrifices, including financial, will be required of all during the period of necessary schooling. Ask yourself why you seek a change. Is it because of disappointment or disillusionment in the present job? Or growing exhilaration in connection with some church work? These may be prompting of the Holy Spirit. List objective results in previous Christian service that affirm God's call. The decision may not come easily or quickly, may involve agony in the constant weighing and reweighing of the data, but will be fulfilling when you find the Lord's will for your career.

As a rule, we should consider ourselves to be God's chosen person occupying the job He has planned for us. One commentator says, "We must believe in God's prudential overruling of our circumstances even before we were converted and therefore, the general rule is to continue in that state of life in which you found yourself when you became a Christian" (Barclay, *A Time to Embrace*, InterVarsity Press, p. 13).

Obedience is Basic

A little girl, told to pick up her toys, replied, "But I want to sing the Doxology." Came the father's reply, "It's no good to praise the Lord while you're in a state of disobedience."

If a student has an evening of homework for tomorrow's assignment, going out to choir practice is not God's will. If we fail to obey in an area in which God's will is clear, we cannot expect further light in unsure areas. If we're not practicing His will today, we shouldn't expect guidance for next week. If we don't follow the light we do have, we'll have darkness. When King Saul persisted in disobedience, "The Lord answered him not, neither by dreams, nor by Urim, nor by prophets." Finally Saul resorted to the witch of Endor for guidance (1 Sam. 28:6-7).

When the people of Judah set up idols in their hearts, then tried to seek the will of the true and living God, they received no answer, but rather suffered a famine of the Word of God (Ezek. 14:1-4; Amos 8:11). A coed who spent her spring vacations living promiscuously on Florida beaches wondered why she couldn't find the will of God for her life.

If we are willing to obey in those matters which we are sure are His will, then He will give light in those areas in which we are not sure. If we do the job at hand, we become available for whatever job He has planned for us later. To those who walk in His way today He will reveal His way tomorrow. The Lord promised to manifest Himself to those that keep His commandments (John 14:21). "In all thy ways acknowledge Him, and He shall direct thy paths" (Prov. 3:6).

The Christian life must be lived faithfully, obeying the responsibility that's now, near, and next.

Little Things Now, Larger Things Later

A young man in seminary was asked to take a Sunday School class. He refused, telling his roommate that he was called to be a preacher, and didn't wish to get involved in so insignificant a matter as a class of children. The young man later discovered the hard way that the Lord doesn't lead to a significant position a person unwilling to do the smaller duty at hand. God promotes to higher positions those faithful in the smaller spots.

The tribes of Ephraim and Manasseh complained to Joshua that, because of the inhabitants of the land, they could not possess all their apportioned territory, the rich district north and south of Shechem. Joshua told them, in effect, to make the most of the opportunities they already had, instead of asking for another lot (Josh. 17:15-18). God won't give us more opportunities if we neglect those we already have. Jesus said, "For unto whomsoever much is given, of him shall be much required," and, "He that is faithful in that which is least, is faithful also in much" (Luke 12:48; 16:10).

D. L. Moody didn't start out as a nationally known evangelist. Rather, he began by going out into the streets and alleys to bring children into Sunday School. The first two or three years he attempted to speak in public, his talks were boring. But he would tell children Bible stories. Expanding opportunities to speak came his way, leading on to international renown. Moody said, "I did the best I could. I used the little talent I had, and God kept giving me more talents, and so, let me say, find some work" (D. L. Moody, *New Sermons, Addresses and Prayers,* St. Louis: N. D. Thompson, 1877, pp. 577-578).

A leading executive, lecturing to a class in business college, was asked how he always managed to be on the most important committees, assigned the most interesting and challenging tasks in his company. He replied, "I always try to take the jobs no one else wants—the dirty work. Then I apply myself the very best I can. It's not long before someone notices and taps me for a bigger, more meaningful spot. The people who want to start at the top rarely get there."

Called When Busy
Since the Lord wants us to be doing the duty at hand, it's not surprising He seems to call most of

His servants when they are already busy with a
task. Too often when needing guidance, the temptation is to stop our regular job and seek a sign.
But it's while doing our usual routine that God's
leading most often comes.

Moses was keeping his father-in-law's flock when
God spoke in the burning bush. Samuel was serving
in the temple. David was watching sheep when
called to greater things. The widow of Zarephath
was gathering sticks to cook her last meal when
Elijah came. Elisha was plowing when Elijah passed
by and cast his mantle on him. Amos was following
the flock when the Lord called him. While Zacharias was performing his usual temple duty, God
revealed His will. Matthew was working at his
tax-collecting booth. Peter, Andrew, James, and
John were fishing when the divine call came.
Followers of God in both Old and New Testaments
were men of movement as well as of meditation.
God leads us when we are busy, doing the tasks
we are supposed to be doing. It was while cobbling
shoes at his bench that William Carey heard God's
call to overseas missions.

Lew Gras, owner of an insurance company in
Denver, and for many years chairman of the Board
of Trustees of Conservative Baptist Seminary, was
shy and introverted as a youth. After becoming a
Christian, he felt a desire and an obligation to communicate, and so took courses in public speaking.

In the Navy, when a sailor who gave legal advice
was hospitalized for a long time, Gras quickly
grabbed some books to learn something about legal
matters. When the need arose, he volunteered advice, amazing his superiors who then promoted him.

Later, on the way to the Marshall Islands, he

studied the way reports should be made for the Admiral's office. When his outfit built an airfield on the Islands, he filed a report with his commander who sent it to Admiral Nimitz's office. The Admiral contacted the commander to ask who was responsible for such a thorough report. Again, Gras was promoted.

Back in America after the war he worked for an insurance company. When he saw little prospect of promotion, he studied the insurance business thoroughly, then decided to start his own company. A few weeks after he started his own outfit, the company he had been working for collapsed, confirming as God's will the starting of his new organization which has prospered to this day. Gras says that by always doing well the job at hand he was in the way when the Lord wanted to lead him along.

Beverly Shea puts it, "Serve where you are with all your heart. Do the job before you well, and other opportunities may blossom because of it. God supplies birds with their food, but He does not put it in their nests."

From assignment to assignment God leads His dear children along.

7

A Step at a Time

After Joseph, Mary, and baby Jesus had lived two years in Egypt to escape the wrath of wicked Herod, the angel gave directions for the return journey. "Go into the land of Israel." Though the parents may have wondered, "Where in Israel?" they received just enough light for the next step. And when they took that step, more illumination came. They were warned against returning to Judea and turned toward the district of Galilee, where they settled in Nazareth. But Joseph and Mary were not told in Egypt that Nazareth would be their destination. As they took each step, light for the next move was revealed (Matt. 2:19-23).

No Blueprint of Particulars
Christian teenagers would like to know what and whom and where, God has for them. Though the

Lord may reveal His will in general, He does not give a blueprint of particulars. For example, a high school sophomore may correctly believe God's will for her is the teaching profession. But she will not receive advance information as to what town or school she will teach in, nor what subjects or grades. In fact, she may not yet know what college she will attend, or what major she will take. God does not reveal the future all at once, but as she follows His leading for the present, He will give light for the next step.

Many of God's servants were informed of His ultimate purpose, but without a schedule of events along the way. Abraham was told to go to a land of promise where he would become father of a nation that would bless all the families of the earth. But he went out, "not knowing whither he went" (Heb. 11:8), unaware that he would stop at Haran, Sichem, the plain of Moreh, and Bethel (Gen. 12:1-8).

The children of Israel were told their destination was the Promised Land. But they did not know where their wilderness wanderings would take them.

The Lord told Peter, Andrew, James, and John that they were to be fishers of men but not the details of where, when, and how they would capture men for Christ. Though Peter was given an inkling of how he was to die, he received no guidebook describing exactly how he was to live (John 21:18).

When the disciples in pre-Ascension dialogue with Jesus asked if the restoration of the kingdom was in the divine plan at that time, He replied with His general outline of witness at Jerusalem, then in Judea and in Samaria, and then to the ends of the earth (Acts 1:6-8). But he didn't produce an advance record of the acts of the apostles.

At his conversion, Paul was instructed about his future in general terms: to bear Christ's name before Gentiles, kings, Israelites, and to suffer for His name's sake (Acts 9:15-16). But he was not granted a detailed list of privations nor an itinerary of future missionary journeys and imprisonments in Caesarea and Rome.

Stanley Jones said, "God's guidance is not a searchlight into the distant future, but a lamp unto our feet." As new believers, we learn of our glorious destiny of conformation to the image of Christ, but the timetable of our progress in transformation is unrevealed. We may know He wants us to be a mechanic or an artist, but the exact blueprint will have to wait to be filled in.

It's just as well the Lord leads us step by step. If a girl knew she was to be a teacher in a certain town 10 years hence, she might be tempted to shortcut efforts to get there, by moving to that town prematurely and applying to the Board of Education before securing adequate training.

> He does not lead me year by year,
> Nor even day by day,
> But step by step my path unfolds;
> My Lord directs my way.
> Tomorrow's plans I do not know,
> I only know this minute.
> —Author Unknown

Take the First Step

When Billy Graham was a student at Florida Bible Institute (now Trinity College) in 1936, he was invited by the dean of the school, John Mindar, to preach at Lake Swan. Terrified at the thought, Graham spent an entire night out on a golf course, struggling within himself. He preached. Next summer Mindar suggested Graham take his large Tampa church during his absence. For six weeks Graham prayed, studied and practiced hour after hour, going out into the woods to preach his sermon to the birds, sometimes going over it 50 times before Sunday. Souls were won. Graham was called as associate pastor. In 1940 he enrolled in Wheaton College, graduating three years later to go on to the pastorate, and then to his illustrious career as an evangelist.

A baby's first step draws enthusiastic parental praise. Though wobbly, that step possesses the quality of walking, which is putting one foot in front of the other. Adding more steps will make walking easier, and take the child somewhere. To find God's will requires that first baby step. Succeeding steps should add confidence.

Many have problems finding God's will because they are unwilling to take the first step toward the task at hand. A young lady, who declared God had called her to tutor underprivileged children in a distant city, was asked what tutoring she was doing among the deprived boys and girls in her own home town. When she had to admit she was doing nothing, she saw how illogical her attitude was. Immediately she became a tutor among the local underprivileged. The person who is faithful in taking the first step will find the second easier.

Called to be the emancipator of his people, Moses was given his first command, "Go, return into Egypt: for all the men are dead which sought thy life" (Ex. 4:19). Then Moses took the first step, which led to the Red Sea deliverance and to all the later steps in the journey toward Israel.

Dramatically converted on the Damascus Road, Saul asked what the Lord would have him do. Came the reply, "Arise, and go into the city, and it shall be told thee what thou must do" (Acts 9:6). Paul immediately obeyed. That first step led to a long series of moves in the will of God.

A Chinese proverb says, "A journey of a thousand miles begins with a single step."

We Must Be Moving

It's easier to change the direction of an object if it's moving. A car in motion responds more readily to a turn of the steering wheel than a parked car. The rudder of a ship is ineffective if the vessel is not moving. Faithful performance in your present occupation, whether as student, employee, or homemaker, makes it easier for the Lord to steer you into His next path for you.

When Eleazar, Abraham's servant, was assigned the task of finding a wife for his master's son, Isaac, he traveled to the area of Abraham's people, the city of Nahor in Mesopotamia. By a well where damsels came to draw water, in response to Eleazar's prayer, God indicated a beautiful woman who was just the girl for Isaac. Eleazar was deeply moved and said, "I being in the way, the Lord led me" (Gen. 24:27). God can maneuver us more easily, if we are moving.

Paul's Macedonian vision was not his call to missionary service, for he had already completed his first missionary journey. The vision came on his second journey, when he was temporarily stymied as to his next step. But because Paul was on the move, and had been for years, God gave him guidance in the vision of the man begging to come to Macedonia.

David Livingstone started for China. But the opium war closed the door. Contact with Robert Moffatt, pioneer missionary to South Africa, turned Livingstone toward Africa. God can guide a person who is moving, and blunders a little off course, better than the man who is drifting but scarcely moving. "And thine ears shall hear a word behind thee, saying, 'This is the way, walk ye in it, when ye turn to the right hand, and when ye turn to the left'" (Isa. 30:21). This promise is for people already in motion to assure them that God will keep them on the right path.

One Philadelphia lady, who thought tne Lord wanted her to be a social worker in France, partly because she spoke fluent French, filled out the proper application forms. But she ended up a social worker in French-speaking Quebec. Because she was moving, the Lord was able to guide her.

Light For The Next Step

A few years ago, a group of men were walking late at night from Emmaus to Jerusalem. The path was narrow and stony, filled with holes and rough places. A traveler coming from the other direction spotted a little light that kept shooting out before these men. As the men came closer, he saw that some had small, clay foot-lamps tied around their ankles by straps. Other men carried larger clay lamps by hand, illuminating a few feet of the stony, unsafe path before them. This experience made him think of the verse, "Thy Word is a lamp unto my feet, and a light unto my path" (Ps. 119:105).

When we don't know God's will for the future, it's usually because we don't need to know at that time. We should major in the here-and-now duties. Then God will handle the variables of tomorrow. The more we travel the road of obedience, the farther the horizon is pushed back.

The Wise Men were led to the Christ Child by stages. Guided by the star to Jerusalem, they then sought the advice of authorities, "Where is He that is born King of the Jews? For we have seen His star in the east, and are come to worship him" (Matt. 2:1-2). The learned scribes told King Herod that according to the prophet Micah, Bethlehem was to be His birthplace (vv. 4-6). Following this additional light, the Magi headed for Bethlehem. Along the way, "lo, the star, which they saw in the east, went before them, till it came and stood over where the young child was" (v. 9). Faithfully following the light for each step ahead, they finally were able to fall in adoration before the newborn King.

When prison chains fell off from Peter's hands, enabling him to follow the angel past the first and then the second guards, he had to walk right up to the iron gate before it opened to permit his escape (Acts 12:5-10). Some of life's great opportunities swing open because we have taken a necessary step toward a closed door.

> One step I see before me,
> Tis all I need to see.

The Will of God is Progressive

God's will is not a magic blueprint dropped by a string from the sky, but more like a scroll that unrolls daily, like the message on TV, too big for the screen, which keeps moving down paragraph by paragraph. Elisabeth Elliot titled her book on the will of God, *A Slow and Certain Light*. Sometimes the Lord guides by a dramatic sign, perhaps when important issues are involved; usually He leads in a quiet, progressive manner. One missionary said that God's guidance is not usually a sharp turn, but a slow curve.

So many when asked how they found God's place of service respond, "It was a series of steps." A man in Christian TV traced the chain of events thus, "I was a pastor of a small church. To augment my income I sold radio time for a station. Then they invited me to try out as an announcer. Then I went into TV announcing. Now I manage a TV station."

The children of Israel were led progressively 40 years in a wilderness that included endless deserts with stunted shrubs and plains of sands, as well as a labyrinth of twisted paths through the mountains. To direct them, God used a pillar of cloud by day, and a pillar of fire by night (Ex. 13:21-22). When the cloud moved, that was the signal for Israel to march. When the cloud stopped, so did the Israelites (40:36-38). Without regular schedule they were kept on their toes. Perhaps they stayed only two days in a place, or a month, or a year (Num. 9:22). The Bible lists 42 stations between Egypt and Jordan, likely only a fragmentary record of the places where something significant occurred (Num. 33). With the monotony of a genealogical table we read, "they removed from . . . , and encamped in . . . " Through the years God gave them not only enough manna and enough strength, but also enough light for each day. So today, God will lead His own from station to station, providing light for each stage of the way.

Not as Drastic as They Seem

A missionary who taught Old Testament in a Portuguese seminary, till it was closed by the mission board, then taught Old Testament in a U. S. Christian college. He believed his gift was teaching, his subject the Old Testament, and the location for teaching Old Testament a minor matter.

The traditional concept of "once a missionary always a missionary" needs to be challenged. Missionaries who resign to take a pastorate or executive job in some Christian organization, or to marry, should not be considered dropouts. Missionary resignations do not differ from pastoral changes. The sovereign Spirit may design a ministry to be temporary, but He does insist on a lifetime commitment to doing the will of God.

Dr. and Mrs. Edward Jacques went to Albania, expecting to serve as missionaries there for life. But seven years later, war forced their return to the United States where they had a happy pastorate in Massachusetts. In 1945 they were appointed by the Conservative Baptist Foreign Missionary Society to resume work in Albania, but the strong Marxist regime closed the door.

Then God led them to Naples, Italy, where again they thought they were missionaries for life. But later the Lord led them to CBFMS headquarters in Wheaton, Illinois, as Overseas Secretary for Europe and Asia. Though not on the mission field, they were still in missions.

When asked how they could bear to be off the

mission field, their reply was, "When we were in Albania, we were happy in the will of God. And we were equally happy in the will of God in Massachusetts, and in Naples, and in Wheaton. We have progressively discovered that our life commitment was not to Albania or Wheaton or Italy, not even to missions, but to the will of God. And the will of God is not static but dynamic."

They added, "We are under sealed orders. We can take only one step at a time. After we take that step of obedience, the Lord will show us the next" (Article, "Once A Missionary Always a Missionary?" in *Impact Magazine*, by Dr. Edward Jacques, Feb. 1977, p. 10).

Be Aware of Changes
The progressive, dynamic nature of God's will means that we should be always ready for a possible change of direction. Moses spent the first third of his life at Pharaoh's busy court. The next third he spent on the backside of a quiet desert. The final third he lived a hectic life, leading God's people out of Egyptian bondage and through the wilderness wanderings.

Paul's life had many changes, involving journeys, jailings, beatings, forced farewells, shipwreck, Rome, release, dreaded prison, then execution. His flexibility in change of plans dovetailed with James' advice, "Go to now, ye that say, 'Today or tomorrow we will go into such a city, and continue there a year, and buy and sell, and get gain': Whereas ye know not what shall be on the morrow . . . For that ye ought to say. 'If the Lord will, we shall live, and do this, or that ' " (4:13-15).

John Calvin planned to move from Paris to Strasbourg to devote his life to study. Detoured through Geneva by military operations, he stopped overnight, then settled there for many years. Carey wanted to serve in the South Sea Islands, but he landed in India.

When Eleanor Page lost her husband, an army colonel, she maintained a home for her two children. After they left home, she applied for a staff position with Campus Crusade. Learning of her military background, they assigned her to Washington, D.C. to conduct Bible studies with military wives. There she also had a good influence on congressional wives, and on Julie Eisenhower.

Mrs. Page maintains that if a husband is taken in death, life is not over for the wife. She says, "I believe God had me marry George Page because He wanted me to teach general's wives. Accept that God has taken something out of your life. Don't get morbid or dwell on the past. Don't disappoint Him by telling Him how great things were. Look forward to the next pages in God's plan" (*Moody Monthly*, article, "God is Your Husband" in March, 1976, p. 83-84).

Yes, God leads us on step by step.

8

More Circumstances: Ability and Advice

In today's working world, there are more than 35,000 job titles. How may a person discover which job God wants him to pursue? We have discussed three basic methods: the Word from above, the call from within, and circumstances from without. Sanctified common sense helps put these pieces together.

One major circumstance that often determines God's direction is the task at hand. The doing of first things first leads to the next step, and the next, with God's will progressively unfolding. There are two more factors which help us to find God's will: ability to meet a need, and advice of spiritually wise friends.

Abilities

To appraise the place of abilities in God's plan for your life, here are some simple steps.

Note your interests. People deciding on schools, jobs, and careers should consider not only what they can do, but what they like to do. Job selection based only on one's ability may lead into an unhappy career, which in turn can spill its discontent into family life.

By failing to regard their preferences when contemplating their life work, many have surrendered a chance to do what is pleasurable and have tied themselves down to what is only profitable. On the other hand, a man whose family firm expected him to join them and earn a big salary, deliberately chose a teaching career. Though not wealthy, he enjoys his work.

How wrong to assume that because we enjoy some particular activity it cannot be God's will. God is no cosmic meanie forcing us to do what is distasteful. Isn't it likely that a good God would will for His children those occupations that bring us delight, not misery?

Assess your abilities. We should note those activities, hobbies, and experiences we enjoy most. Do we prefer skills that involve people or paper? Do we like fine arts, traveling, physical exercise, animals, books, history, politics, machines, research, administration, writing, teaching, accounting?

If you have just one arm, the Lord isn't likely leading you to be a violin player. If you can't pass chemistry, medicine is probably not your field. If you have a poor voice, singing is not your career. If you want to play tackle for the Pittsburgh Steelers but weigh only 150 pounds, think again. If you cannot design, God's will is likely not architecture.

A missionary claimed God's will was Venezuela, but his family doctor insisted his wife could not take the climate there. The missionary said he would trust the Lord, but he had to return permanently because of her health.

It isn't enough to have an interest in something. We must make sure it fits our capabilities. So we must evaluate our personality traits, talents, technical skills, and spiritual gifts. (See "How to Discover Your Gifts" in *19 Gifts of the Spirit*, Flynn, p. 192, Victor Books). Batteries of aptitude and psychological tests are available today which can help an individual discover his area of competence. For example, Christian Vocations and Testing, P.O. Box 542, Wheaton, Illinois, has information on aptitude tests and current job opportunities in both Christian and secular careers.

Common sense plays a part. Does a potential line of work make use of your talents? Are you fit physically? Nate Saint, jungle pilot martyred by the Aucas, used to say, "Have you noticed that when a man finds the will of the Lord for his life there always seems to be an evident relationship between the talents or gifts or preparation the Lord has given him, and the job the Lord has called him to do?"

God doesn't ask the toe to see, nor the eye to walk. His plan will be in accord with our makeup and endowments.

Experiment with activities. A girl with a mild interest in music tried out for a girls' trio, but never got the part. But given a role in the college play, she discovered genuine dramatic ability. We ought to diversify our activities and dabble in new avenues. As the TV commercial said, "Try it; you may like it."

Though God usually leads in the realm of natural abilities, there are exceptions. Most folks would never have encouraged stuttering Demosthenes to become an orator. But the Lord may call a person to do something for which he does not seem fitted, in which case He will give the necessary endowment. How unlikely that shoe salesman D. L. Moody seemed destined to be a world-renowned preacher, or baseball player Billy Sunday a sawdust-trail evangelist.

But more often than not, God directs a person to a task for which he has the basic qualification, and in which he shows some degree of effectiveness.

Develop your capabilities. Possession of a gift is a call to perfect it. "Neglect not the gift that is in thee" (1 Tim. 4:14). Cultivation may mean trade school, college training, even grad school. Or it may require informal training at home by correspondence, or evening adult courses.

Not only preparation but persistence is needed. In the secular world, Abraham Lincoln, Louis Pasteur, and Thomas Edison did not give up in despair after initial failure. Recognition of our abilities as God-given will help us overcome obstacles and adverse circumstances, not overnight, but through enduring patience.

Meet needs. Naturally, we do not choose what we think is God's place of service on the basis of need, for then everyone would have to rush to the same pockets of privation. Nor do we try to fill every need, or we would be victimized by every sad situation, dissipating our energies in a hundred directions. It is the sovereign Lord who decides where we labor, but usually He assigns us to a place where our abilities can fill a need.

When God gave directions for the building of the tabernacle, a need arose for men with special ability in stonecutting, wood carving, curtain making, and "in all manner of workmanship." God provided many divinely skilled workmen, led by Bezaleel and Aholiab, who clearly fulfilled His will by making all the necessary items (Ex. 31:1-11). The same situation existed 500 years later when skillful men were needed for the decorative work in Solomon's temple (2 Chron. 2:13-14).

After Chuck Colson was released from prison, he was praying as to his future ministry. Suddenly a prison door opened to him which had not been open to outsiders for two years. Then another door, permitting him to go into the Federal Prison System. His own experience as a convict enabled him to understand the needs of these men.

If a need begins to burden your heart, and you develop the conviction that you have the ability to do something about it, this may well be God speaking to you.

Possess a sense of mission. Though the overarching mission of every Christian life should be the evangelization of the lost and the discipling of the saved, this does not mean that everyone will be a full-time Christian worker. Perhaps jobs can be divided into three major types: secular, full-time Christian service, and supportive.

The secular world. Unless strongly led otherwise, many Christian career guides suggest secular employment for most people, but with the urging to participate actively during free time in Christian work, through church and related organizations. The Lord calls to secular jobs as well as to the so-called sacred. The consistent believer can be

God's person in the secular world, considering his career a divine calling.

Full time. Pastors, assistant pastors, missionaries, music directors, Christian Ed directors, come under this category, to name a few.

Supportive. These are full-time jobs within Christian organizations where the main responsibility is other than sharing God's Word in personal contact. For example, office worker, secretary, accountant, editor, artist, houseparent, dietician, mechanic, pilot.

INTERCRISTO, P. O. Box 1323, Seattle, WA 98109, published a 781 page *Directory of Christian Work Opportunities* in 1977, listing over 18,000 Christian personnel openings worldwide. This organization also offers INTERMATCH, an individual, custom service to help match up people's abilities to openings around the world. In recent years, overseas missionary societies have come to utilize hundreds of specially skilled homeland people from teenage to retirement, who hold down secular jobs, but who give short-term service abroad.

Because too often the Christian community acts as if secular jobs belong to a second-class category, it needs to be emphasized that secular and supportive tasks are as spiritual as full-time vocations. If our calling is God's will, then our job is as holy as that of a preacher or missionary.

Advice of Fellow Believers
As members of the body of Christ, we are to counsel one another. Fellow believers may be a channel of direction through their insight and input.

Incidentally, the advice of authority is usually

God's will for us. Children are not to despise
parental advice, for it comes out of much experience and the desire to save offspring from mistakes (Prov. 15:5; 23:22-23). Children are also
under teachers, then later under employers, as well
as under the law of the land. The census decree of
Caesar Augustus was the will of God to bring
Joseph and Mary to Bethlehem so the prophecy
of Jesus' birthplace could be fulfilled. Except where
dictum conflicts with the Word of God, Christian
duty must accept the rule of authorities as the will
of God (Rom. 13:1).

Books may well contain written wisdom from
men that will prove helpful in decision-making. At
the last Urbana Missionary Conference (1976), a
wide variety of workshops provided opportunities
for guidance in youthful lives.

Seek the counsel of friends. When Edwin Frizen
was approached about taking the position of Executive Director of the International Foreign Mission
Association (IFMA), he enlisted the prayer support
of his pastor in Minneapolis, and a godly uncle and
aunt. Within a few days, both pastor and relatives
stopped on a trip south to see him at Florida State
University where he was taking graduate studies.
Says Frizen, "The Lord enabled us to have the
personal counsel of these close prayer partners at
a time when we had no idea they would be in
Florida, and when we had to make an important
career decision." Frizen has been IFMA Executive
Director since 1963.

Find someone you can consult. Talking your
thoughts out with a friend often helps to clarify
the fuzzy areas. Paul chose Timothy because he
was "well reported of by the brethren that were at

Lystra and Iconium" (Acts 16:2). The advice of friends restrained Paul from rushing into the tumultuous amphitheatre at Ephesus where rioting shrinemakers might easily have harmed him, because of severe decrease in their business due to the apostle's preaching (Acts 19:30-31).

When a church looking for a pastor received the same recommendation from three separate sources, they accepted the agreement as divine confirmation. A happy pastorate ensued. "In the multitude of counselors there is safety" (Prov. 11:14).

Many men received part of God's direction for their lives through the advice of friends. Soon after his conversion, Jack Wyrtzen became acquainted with Percy Crawford of "Young People's Church of the Air" fame. Sensing Wyrtzen's potentialities, Crawford urged him to go 100 percent into youth evangelism and to use radio as his pulpit. So Wyrtzen launched a Gospel broadcast on a small station. Through the years he has maintained a coast-to-coast broadcast plus his mammoth Word Of Life Camp and other ministries.

Herbert J. Taylor, for many years president of Club Aluminum, faced an important decision in his early business life. Offered a good position in industry, he was also offered a more tempting job with the YMCA. He sought the advice of a Christian friend who said, "You think I'm going to tell you to go with the YMCA, don't you? That's because you love young people—it's probably your first love. I suggest you go into business. First, I think you'll be a success. Second, use all of your extra time to work with youth. As time goes by, I believe you'll be successful enough in business to have your own company. You'll be able to take time away from business for your youth activities. By the time you're 45, you'll be spending more of your time on young people's projects than on your business. In the last few years of your life, I believe you'll be working full-time at it."

The advice proved accurate. Taylor became a renowned industrialist, authored the famous "Four-Way Test," and pioneered in the founding and development of many well-known Christian youth organizations, including Christian Service Brigade, Pioneer Girls, Inter-Varsity, Young Life, and National Child Evangelism Fellowship (Herbert J. Taylor with Robert Walker, *God Has A Plan For You*, Creation House, 1972, pp. 22-23).

The Lord should speak to others on mutual matters. Dr. Paul Little said, "I get very suspicious of people who come with very pious and spiritual language, telling me that God has led them to do some wild, outlandish thing, and nobody else has gotten the message. Undoubtedly, God may in rare instances guide us in a way that is totally contrary to the thinking of equally committed Christians, but I think it would be the rare exception rather than the rule."

A well-known evangelistic song leader was followed around every summer from Bible conference to Bible conference by a lady who claimed that the Lord had told her he was to marry her. Commented the song leader, "The Lord hasn't told me."

When a married man thinks the Lord is calling him into the ministry, he should consult with his wife, for if she feels no call to be a pastor's wife, their marriage may be headed for trouble.

When we think God is leading us, the counsel of saints who are equally committed to the will of

God can be a confirming or negating factor. It was as *they*, a group of leaders, ministered to the Lord and fasted that divine guidance came to separate Barnabas and Saul for the first missionary journey (Acts 13:2). The verdict of the first church council was carried to the churches with this comment, "It seemed good to the Holy Ghost, *and to us*" (Acts 15:28). The Lord usually communicates the same advice to others as He does to us. That's why would-be seminary students are asked to provide the endorsement of their home church, and missionary candidates must secure the approval of a mission board before comissioning for overseas service.

The writer of Proverbs said, "Don't go ahead with your plans without the advice of others" (20:18, LB).

Seek the advice of spiritual friends. In the secular world you consult the experts for advice, for example, a lawyer when you need legal counsel. In Christian matters, seek the suggestion of Christian brothers, not nonbelievers who usually do not understand why a person should "waste his life" in overseas missionary work when he could make it big financially in his home country.

The disastrous advice to increase taxes given Rehoboam by nonspiritual advisors resulted in the division of the kingdom of Israel into the northern and southern domains. He should have listened to the counsel of mature men at court (1 Kings 12:1-15). "Blessed is the man that walketh not in the counsel of the ungodly" (Ps. 1:1). But "he that walketh with wise men [who are sensitive to spiritual realities and objectives] shall be wise" (Prov. 13:20).

Listen to advice with humility. If a nominating

committee of many members, after deliberation and prayer, puts up your name for deacon or trustee, you'd better think twice before you refuse to run.

The owner of a Christian TV station auditions programs to find those professionally acceptable for airing on his station. Often, when he gives suggestions for improvement, the producers egotistically refuse it. He comments, "If they are in the will of God, they should be willing to accept advice." For a person to refuse counsel is like a girl saying "God is leading me to be a secretary but I refuse any lessons on typing."

"The way of a fool is right in his own eyes: but he that hearkeneth unto counsel is wise" (Prov. 12:15).

Don't let others decide for you. In the final analysis *you* have to make the decision. Advice from Christian friends, even the pastor, must be measured by the Word of God, the voice of the Spirit, and day-by-day fellowship with Christ. Each person is responsible to the Lord and must decide for himself (Rom. 14:3-5).

Christian friends may be wrong. On one occasion Paul had to reject the insistent advice of well-meaning associates. With deep love for his fellow Israelites, hope of winning many to Christ, and desire to bind the Gentile churches to the mother church at Jerusalem, he planned to go to Jerusalem, carrying the offering from Gentile converts to needy Jews there (Acts 19:21; 20:16).

Along the way, he was repeatedly warned of deep sufferings that would befall him at Jerusalem (Acts 20:23; 21:4, 10-11). When loving believers weepingly begged him not to proceed, he replied, " 'What mean ye to weep and to break mine heart? For I am ready not to be bound only, but also to die at Jerusalem for the name of the Lord Jesus.' And when he would not be persuaded, we [friends] ceased, saying, 'The will of the Lord be done'" (Acts 21:13-14).

Some believe Paul stepped out of the will of God in proceeding to Jerusalem in the face of repeated warnings. Yet Paul strongly declared that he "went bound in the Spirit into Jerusalem" (Acts 20:22). Was Paul in the will of God or not?

The explanation seems to be that the prediction of suffering was indeed inspired by the Spirit, but that the advice not to go to the holy city was a human interference. Certain persons, exercising their Spirit-given gifts, correctly foresaw the painful consequences of his going, but then incorrectly added, without the Spirit's direction, their personal persuasions. The leading given Paul's friends concerned only information; the leading given Paul concerned his duty. Though right in seeing what would happen, they were wrong in urging against his trip. Paul was right in resisting their counsel, for the will of God did take him to Jerusalem. Vindication seemingly came to Paul one night in the Jerusalem prison when the Lord said, "Be of good cheer, Paul: for as thou hast testified of Me in Jerusalem, so must thou bear witness also at Rome" (Acts 23:11).

Elisabeth Elliot found the above incident from Paul's life helpful when she felt led to move to Auca territory with her little girl, and live there, for almost unanimously, close friends responded with alarm. She was forced to weigh again all the evidence, realize the risks, count the cost, and pray. Though she took others into her confidence, yet she knew the final decision was hers. God blessed her two-year stay in Auca land, but the decision was no easy matter.

Each believer should contemplate the counsel of others, but refuse to be controlled by it. The voice of the Spirit must take priority over the voice of friends.

9

Delay
and Pray

A Christian received a phone call from a certain company, inviting him to take a position with them. Taken back by surprise, he replied, "I'll have to pray about it."

Came the answer, "I'll hold the phone."

The Principle of Delay

We should guard against snap judgments and hasty decisions. When Dale Evans needs guidance, she ponders the problem, prays over it, commits it to the Lord, then sleeps on it, sometimes dismissing it for awhile, knowing the Lord will give direction in His good time.

Even when a matter has been tentatively decided, it's wise to sit on it, delay implementation, not even share it except with a trusted friend. Otherwise it's difficult, even embarrassing, to reverse that decision.

A pastor accepted a call to head a Christian organization, only to resign two months later because he found out management was not God's will.

If to delay is wise strategy when your mind is 95 percent made up, how much wiser to wait if in doubt. When unsure about making a change in the area of marital status, job, housing, car, or an expensive purchase, it's better to maintain the status quo than to hurry into a disastrous mistake. "It is dangerous and sinful to rush into the unknown" (Prov. 19:2, LB). Rather, we should "wait on the Lord" till positive leading comes (Ps. 37:34; 40:1; Isa. 40:31). The period of delay may vary from minutes to months.

The saintly George Muller said, "Never be in a hurry in deciding questions of great importance." A business friend asked his counsel on a matter that had to be decided that morning. When Muller replied that he could not see him till evening, the man said the matter could not wait, for the opportunity of making thousands of dollars had to be accepted by noon. Muller advised him to decline the offer, for anything that did not permit proper time to consult God was not likely of God. The friend rejected Muller's advice in favor of the tempting venture, but in six months was a ruined man.

The old divines used to say that whenever God speaks to us about anything, He always gives us time to recognize His voice.

When an Israeli youth blasphemed the name of the Lord, "they put him in ward, that the mind of the Lord might be shewed them" (Lev. 24:12).

When the Sanhedrin deliberated the fate of the disciples who had filled all Jerusalem with Gospel doctrine, venerable Gamaliel advised delay of verdict, reasoning that if the prisoners' work was of man it would come to nothing, but if of God, it could not be stopped (Acts 5:38-39). Says the proverb, "Time will tell."

Any couple trying to determine if their romance is true love or mere infatuation should give it time. True love grows with the passing of time. Many who fell in love at first sight wish they had taken a second look. The best advice for couples in doubt is to delay marriage. Time will test their compatibility.

Elisabeth Elliot told the 17,000 students at Urbana '76 that when Jim Elliot told her one week before her college graduation that he loved her, he went on to say that he hadn't the least inkling that God wanted him to marry her. They waited five years before they were married.

If no mate is in sight, a Christian should not be prematurely preoccupied with thoughts of romance and marriage. Rather than letting such obsessive thoughts handicap his Christian life, he should wait on God to send along the right one in His perfect timing. And if there is to be no mate, God's will should be accepted.

God Leads in Delays

God's schedule differs from ours. We cannot impose our time limits on God. Though we may wish an answer by a certain date, we must learn to wait confidently in His timing. A long delay does not mean a lack of God's interest.

The stops—as well as the starts—of a good man are ordered by the Lord. The red traffic lights which cause us to stop guide as much as the green lights which permit us to go. Guidance may be to wait as well as to proceed. When the Israelites were halted in the same place for several weeks, they were receiving guidance, just as clearly as when the cloud moved and directed them onward.

To move forward before God so signals is to run ahead of God. Instead of waiting God's time, Abraham brought a son into the world through Sarah's handmaiden. The animosity between the half brothers, Ishmael and Isaac, persists today in the Israeli-Arab controversy (Gen. 16).

Moses moved prematurely to be his people's emancipator from Egypt, but had to flee into a 40-year exile before God's time came for him to lead the Israelites out of Egyptian bondage (Acts 7:23-36).

After the capture of Jericho, Joshua was visited by a delegation of Gibeonites, disguised as ambassadors from a far country. Fooled, he rushed into a league of peace, only to discover three days later that he had been duped into a premature pact (Josh. 9:1-16).

At times, of course, a decision must be made quickly. But on occasions that permit pause, it's better to wait and secure a proper perspective than to rush in and create havoc.

God Works Behind the Scenes

When Naomi saw that her daughter-in-law Ruth had done all she could in her situation with their nearest kinsman, Boaz, she gave her this advice, "Sit still, my daughter, until thou know how the matter will fall" (Ruth 3:18). So Ruth waited. The result was marriage to Boaz, and progenitorship of David.

Though David, already anointed king, became a hero by slaying giant Goliath, he made no rush to take the throne from Saul. Rather, he "behaved himself wisely in all his ways" (1 Sam. 18:14). On two occasions David could have killed sleeping Saul, but he refused to stretch forth his hand against the Lord's anointed. He let God end Saul's life in His divine time. In God's scheduling David was ultimately elevated to a long and successful reign.

A teenage boy was refused admission to the college of his choice because he was under age, according to their regulation. Though offered acceptance by another college, he waited two years till admitted by the college he believed was God's will. When a senior, he spotted the girl who later became his wife. Since she was a freshman, he would not likely have met her, apart from his two-year delay.

When his donkeys wandered away, Kish sent his son Saul to search for them. On the third day Saul met Samuel. What a memorable day for Saul, for not only did Samuel inform him that the donkeys had been found, but he also told him he was to be the king of Israel. The first two days had passed uneventfully for Saul, dusty, dry, and donkeyless. But God was working during the delay of those two days, instructing Samuel, guiding Saul, to make all things work out beautifully for that thrilling third day (1 Sam. 9).

A man impulsively left his place of employment one afternoon, intending to tell his boss next morning that he was quitting. Though well suited to the job, he was finding no satisfaction. That evening he had an appointment with a Christian counselor who advised him to resume his job in the morning and wait on God for direction. Two weeks later the boss called him into his office to say, "For several weeks now I've been thinking of creating a new position that would be just the spot for you." He took the new job, finding great satisfaction therein.

The eager hurry in people who rush to a quick decision may be a red light to warn that the move is not of the Spirit. God never makes mistakes, but we often do when we act with too much haste. A denominational leader suggested that a pulpit committee could well take more time to seek spiritual guidance in the choice of a new pastor, thus sparing the church the agonies of having to sever the relationship later.

A faithful deacon was pacing the floor like a caged lion. "What's the trouble?" someone asked. Sensing his own problem, he answered, "I'm in a hurry and God isn't!"

God's direction often comes more as a gentle nudge than a vigorous push. The Psalmist said, "My soul waiteth for the Lord more than they that watch for the morning" (Ps. 130:6). Light may come gradually, almost imperceptibly, ever so slowly, but dawn will come, illuminating our path.

Pray for God's Guidance
Before the time of modern navigational aids, a traveler crossing the Atlantic noticed the boat had two compasses. One was fixed to the deck, easily seen by the man at the wheel, while the other compass was fastened high up on a mast which a sailor would periodically climb in order to take a reading. When the passenger asked why two com-

passes, the captain explained, "This is an iron vessel. The compass on deck is sometimes affected by its surroundings, but the compass on the mast is above influence. So we steer by the compass above."

Though God has given us minds to use so that many matters can be decided by common sense, we need to remind ourselves that our reason, victimized by our sinful nature, is not infallible. So we should lift our hearts in prayer for guidance from the compass above. As Proverbs says, "Trust in the Lord with all thine heart; and lean not unto thine own understanding" (3:5). Just as the judges in Israel decided small matters themselves but took the hard cases to Moses, so, too, when we face decisions too difficult for solving by our reason, we should seek wisdom from a higher court (Ex. 18:25-26). But we never need pray for God's will on anything in which the Bible has already clearly spoken.

When famine hit Canaan, Abraham went down to sojourn in Gerar without consulting God, and got into trouble. Isaac did the same thing several years later (Gen. 20; 26:6-11).

When a Christian leader immediately turned down an invitation to a position of leadership offered him by a Christian organization, a close friend present during the conversation later commented, "I wonder about the way you answered those men. You didn't pray about it."

Eleazar in his assignment to find a wife for Isaac, lifted his heart in prayer for help (Gen. 24:12).

Repeatedly, David asked direction of the Lord before pursuing a course of action (2 Sam. 2:1; 5:19, 23). He probably summoned the high priest, who functioned as the mouthpiece of God. Many psalms include prayers for guidance like David's, "Lead me, and guide me" (31:3).

Commands to Seek Guidance

Jesus told His followers to ask, seek, and knock, and they would receive an answer (Matt. 7:7-8). Among the good gifts of the Heavenly Father is guidance. No detail of a problem is too small to pray about: where will the money come from, who will mind the children, how long should the trip be, who will take our Pioneer Girls those few weeks?

Jesus spent a night in prayer before selecting His disciples. We may need a quiet place and time so that our minds may be clear and judgment unwarped, as we seek His light for an important verdict.

When the disciples had to decide who would take the place of Judas among the Twelve, they nominated two qualified candidates, then prayed, "Thou, Lord, who knowest the hearts of all men, show which one of these two Thou hast chosen" (Acts 1:24, NASB).

Certainly, guidance itself is something we can pray for. "Let your requests be made known unto God" (Phil. 4:6). "Let us therefore come boldly unto the throne of grace, that we may obtain mercy, and find grace to help in time of need" (Heb. 4:16). "If any of you lack wisdom, let him ask of God . . . and it shall be given him" (James 1:5). The *Living Bible* puts it, "If you want to know what God wants you to do, ask Him, and He will gladly tell you."

One man said that often in his extremity he

looks up, and in audible voice asks. "What should I do? You're right here with me. You know all the angles. Please tell me the best approach at this point."

Johann Gutenberg, who printed the first Bible in the 15th century, had been seeking a way to overcome the tedious process of copying lengthy manuscripts by hand. When he received the idea of using movable type, he exclaimed to his associates, "To work, then! God has revealed to me the secret I demanded of Him."

Paul Little, when a student, had been rushing around campus, going to this meeting and that, talking to everyone under the sun, reading this book and that book, trying to learn everyone's formula for the will of God. At Urbana Missionary Convention in 1948, a missionary from India asked, "You who are so concerned about the will of God, how many of you have spent just five minutes a day asking God to show you what His will is?" Said Little, "I was frustrated out of my mind trying to find God's will. I was doing everything but getting into His presence and asking Him to show me. It is remarkable how God answers prayer in this particular area, as well as in others."

Herbert J. Taylor, president of Club Aluminum for many years, and author of the famous "Four-Way Test," said the four principles came to him in answer to prayer for God's guidance in formulating basic policies for his company.

Fasting and Prayer
Some have found that fasting, along with prayer, has helped bring divine leading. To fast is to voluntarily abstain from food. But it's more than

just not eating. It's a means of seeking God for a special spiritual guidance. Ezra proclaimed a fast when he needed to know a route by which a group of captives could safely travel from Persia to Jerusalem (Ezra 8:21).

Fasting and prayer are often linked in the Bible, as in the case of Cornelius, and in the appointment of Barnabas and Saul for missionary work (Acts 10:30; 13:3-4). Fasting shifts attention from temporal to eternal matters. Making up your mind not to eat keeps before you the reason you are foregoing nourishment. The heavenly Father notes the concentrated attention toward Him which, along with the praying, signals the seriousness of purpose in His child.

When a decision doesn't come easily, it may be that we are harboring wrong motives. Prayer may help us spot our own rationalizations. Are we bringing to this decision factors of envy, escapism, ego-boosting, arrogance, power-seeking, or self-indulgence? Young people sometimes hurry into marriage, propelled by a sense of well-being, when in reality it's a chemical balance that makes them feel euphoric. Prayer helps us to say, "Search me, O God, and know my heart: try me, and know my thoughts: and see if there be any wicked way in me, and lead me into the way everlasting" (Ps. 139:23-24).

When Dr. Billy Melvin was invited to become the Executive Director of the National Association of Evangelicals, he found it quite a struggle to know what to do. In his current assignment as a denominational executive, he had just completed a lovely new office building for all departments of the work, he was experiencing a satisfying sense

of momentum, and he had also just completed a
new home. At the same time, he knew the importance of NAE to the evangelical cause. This overwhelming conviction caused him to resign and
move to NAE headquarters in Wheaton, but only
after three months of much prayer.

Beverly Shea says that one of the most difficult
letters to answer is one asking for career advice,
mainly because he himself did not take full, formal
schooling. The first point he tries to make is, "Pray
that God will direct your path. The most important
question you can ask yourself is if God wants it for
you."

Just before Shea went to the platform during a
crusade, a teenage girl asked, "How do I get into
this business? My friends say I wow 'em when I
sing a hymn." Thrown by her brashness, but trying
not to show it, Shea replied, "Let me ask you a
question. Do you want to sing for the Lord or for
yourself? You must decide which it is to be. You
pray about it."

After the service, as he was leaving the platform,
Shea was approached by a young man who asked,
"Tell me, Mr. Shea, how do you choose that song
you sing just before Mr. Graham preaches—
through prayer?" Shea told him he always looked
to the Lord for guidance in choosing songs. The
boy smiled, "I thought so. I love to sing too, Mr.
Shea, and some day I hope I'll be doing what you
are. Pray that God will lead me." This attitude
warmed Shea's heart. (Story from book by Beverly
Shea with Fred Bauer, *Then Sings My Soul*, Revell,
1971, pp. 139-141).

When George Muller was faced with a decision
on the will of God, he so often responded, "I cannot

give you an answer now, but I will let you know after I have considered the matter prayerfully." It was: delay—and pray. (Robert Steer, *George Muller, Delighted in God,* Harold Shaw Publishers, Wheaton, IL 1975, p. 24).

Meditative prayer helps bring our wills into harmony with His will, giving us the confidence "that, if we ask anything according to His will, He heareth us" (1 John 5:14).

10

Fleece, Faith, and Peace

Fascinated by the story of Gideon's fleece, some people wonder if they should seek an unusual sign at a crossroad of life to determine God's will. One fellow, to solve puzzling problems, would pray, "Lord, if it is Your will, may the light at the next corner stay green till I get there." Another, facing a crucial decision, asked the Lord to give guidance by making his phone ring at 9:20 P.M. Is "putting out the fleece" a legitimate way of ascertaining the divine will?

The situation in Gideon's case was precarious. The Midianites had chased the Israelites into mountain caves, stripped their fields of harvest, withdrawn into their own country, and were threatening again. Gideon's decision was of enormous consequence.

No one should ever "play the game of Gideon's

fleece" on inconsequential matters. "Putting out a fleece" can be used as an excuse to avoid coming to grips with the issue and to escape commitment to do what is right. We should never trifle with God, nor try to see Him work just for our amazement. Also, if God has already spoken clearly on a matter in the Bible, there is no point to further seek His will.

For Confirmation, Not Direction

When the Lord told Gideon he was to save Israel from the hand of the Midianites, Gideon requested a sign. The Lord responded by sending a fire to consume Gideon's sacrifice. Then Gideon wanted more confirmation. He asked that the fleece of wool, put out in the evening, be wet in the morning but with the surrounding ground dry. The next day he was able to wring out a bowl full of water from the fleece; the ground around the fleece was dry. Then Gideon reversed the test, asking for a dry fleece next morning, and wet ground. And it was so (Judges 6:11-40).

Note that Gideon had already been clearly directed what to do before he put out the fleece. In fact, he had already taken a step of obedience by sounding the trumpet to gather his army. Yet he still had difficulty believing God would use *him* to save Israel. So the fleece test really had nothing to do with discerning God's will, but rather was a request for verification of direction already given —to make sure he had heard correctly.

Test of variation. Since God had spoken with certainty about Gideon's forthcoming victory, the fleece test indicates doubt of the divine call. Even after the first test had been met, Gideon apologetically said, in effect, "Don't get angry with me, but I want another proof. This time reverse things." He was asking for what is known in experimental science as the test of variation, where one reverses the order of things to verify results.

To demand a miracle, or the unusual, may indicate deficiency of faith, and may also come under the Saviour's censure, "Except ye see signs and wonders, ye will not believe" (John 4:48), and "An evil and adulterous generation seeketh after a sign" (Matt. 12:39). Zacharias, when told he would become a father, was stricken dumb because in unbelief he asked for a sign (Luke 1:18-20). In contrast, the Virgin Mary, when told she was to have a baby, asked for no sign, but in faith submitted, "Be it unto me according to thy word" (1:38).

God is under no obligation to answer. When Gideon proposed the test, God was not obligated to answer. We cannot put a sovereign God in a corner, or in a box, or issue Him deadlines. If we give Him a hot potato, He may refuse to handle it. Who are we to dictate to Deity an arbitrary course of action in order to give us direction? When Satan asked Jesus to put His heavenly Father to the test by jumping off the temple pinnacle, Jesus replied that it was wrong to tempt God (Matt. 4:7).

In marvelous kindness, God came to Gideon's place of need and answered him. However, in the Bible signs of this type were not often given. Today, God can and does show His will by signs, on rare occasions. They are the exceptions, gifts of His grace, and are not available on demand. We have three gifts that Gideon did not possess: a long history of God dealing with His people, the complete Scriptures, and the indwelling Holy Spirit.

A fleece should involve common sense, circumstances, or advice. Gideon's fleece had little connection with the deliverance of Israel from the Midianites. For what connection is there between a fleece and fighting? Acceptable fleeces in our day would bear some relationship to common sense, circumstances, or advice.

Creatures made in the image of God should exercise reason and common sense in putting out a fleece, rather than seeking meaningless signs or making irresponsible demands on God.

Eleazar, in searching for a wife for Isaac, put out a fleece. Waiting by a well in Abraham's native city of Nahor, he asked the Lord to have the woman of His choice offer a drink, not only to him, but to his camels as well. This wasn't a wild, irrational stipulation, for he not only wanted Isaac to have a pretty wife, but one who was also strong and industrious—which would be demonstrated in the strenuous task of fetching enough water to supply the thirst of 10 camels (Gen. 24:10, 14).

A man considering a change of job needed a year's special training. When two colleges turned him down, he put out the fleece, "Lord, if You are in my proposed change of job, please give me reassurance by having this next college accept me speedily." In addition to accepting him immediately, they offered him a scholarship as well.

When the late Dr. M. R. DeHaan, originator of the Radio Bible Class, felt God calling him to give up his medical practice to preach, he realized that his testimony as a professional man might be greater if he remained in practice, so he put out a fleece. He advertised in the American Medical

Association's journal a high sale figure for his new home and large practice, telling Mrs. DeHaan, "If there's a buyer, it could only be the Lord's doing." In two days, 60 doctors responded, with DeHaan selling to the first applicant. Such a fleece is in essence a strong circumstance that helps the pieces fall together in one coherent plan.

When George Muller was young, he was not well, and his friends advised him to go to the country for a change of air. Muller prayed, "Lord, if Thou wilt have me go, let me know by the answer of my doctor. If in reply to my question he says it would be very good for me, I will go; but if he says it is of not great importance, then I will stay." The doctor's verdict was, "It is the very best thing you could do." So he went. That type of fleece really boils down to advice of a competent friend, certainly a type of circumstance that helps us find God's will. (See chapter 8.)

Scholars differ as to the legitimacy of the fleece method today. Those who recognize it usually restrict its use to matters of major import. No miracle involving the suspension of the laws of nature should be demanded. Rather, any stipulation should be reasonable, the fulfillment of which would provide, not so much the discerning of God's will, but circumstantial verification of direction already given. Though God sometimes concedes to our inability to discover God's will by condescending to answer the demands of our fleece, He is under no obligation to answer, and nowhere suggests we seek such a sign.

Faith, Not Fleece

An air traffic controller at O'Hare Airport in Chicago felt a call to the ministry. His conviction was fed by an awareness of the masses of people at the airport who, though directed to physical safety by the controllers, were still lost and unsafe, apart from Christ. A bachelor with two cars, some stocks and plenty of insurance, he figured that to finance his college education after resigning his airport position, he would have to sell most of his assets and then would still need to have $50 per week.

So he put out a fleece. He told the Lord he would contact the college of his choice, and ask if it would be possible to go to college full-time and also get a job paying $50 a week. If the answer were yes, he would take that as God's will to go. If no, he would know that it was not His will. The college informed him that such a thing could not be done.

But was No really God's answer? He wondered, "Who am I to tell God that He has to prove ahead of time His ability to provide for me? How can I preach about faith to others, if I don't have faith myself?"

So he resigned his job. His first Sunday at college he received a preaching assignment in a nearby town. The treasurer handed him a check for $50. He continued preaching there for a year till a regular pastor was called. Then he preached in a small church, receiving $35 a week, which he found sufficient. During the summer he returned to the control tower at O'Hare with a pay increase; it was the first time under Federal Aviation that anyone was permitted to work in the control tower on a part-time basis. He learned that God did not have to prove in advance that He could take care of him.

God hides His will to develop faith. There is no foolproof formula that automatically produces God's will. God never makes His will so clear that a believer walks completely by sight. God wants us to step out in faith. Only in retrospect can we have some measure of certainty that our course of action was in the divine will.

When we seem guided into a path that mystifies our shortsightedness, we can trust that our all-wise God knows what path is best for us in the long run. Does He not know the end from the beginning? A fellow wondered why God's leading seemed to take him to an architectural school, then a business college, then a seminary. He had his answer years later when he became director of a Bible conference, for he had to design new buildings, supervise all business dealings, and oversee the theological direction of the program.

In ancient times, a servant looked constantly toward his master for any silent or subtle signal, like a glance of the eye. Similarly, we must ever look in the direction of our Master, for He has promised to guide us with His eye (Ps. 32:8). He wants us to be more interested in the Planner than in the plan. One man who has tried to follow God's will for the last 30 years claims it is still the full-time job it was three decades ago, ever requiring daily faith. Our search for God's will continues all through life.

Act in Faith

We never hesitate to start down an unknown highway even though we have no way of foreseeing all the detours, rough spots, curves, hills, heavy traffic and "under repair" areas. We begin with faith that we'll reach our destination. Before the Israelites crossed into the Promised Land, Moses gave this encouragement, "And the Lord, He it is that doth go before thee; He will be with thee, He will not fail thee, neither forsake thee: fear not, neither be dismayed" (Deut. 31:8).

David Brainerd, who died at 29 carrying the Gospel to the Indians of New England in an itinerant ministry, wrote,

> I go on not knowing,
> I would not, if I might;
> I'd rather walk in the dark with God
> Than go alone in the light;
> I'd rather walk by faith with Him
> Than go alone with sight.

Sometimes a fear of making a mistake paralyzes people into inaction. If you must decide by Monday, and Monday rolls around without electrifying experience or clear guidance, you assess all the factors, trust God to guide in your decision, then launch out in faith, "Lord, this is the way I see it. I go ahead in confidence." Then, having put your hand to the plow, faith should not look back but go forward in the task.

Dr. Vernon Grounds, president of Denver Seminary for two decades, recounts that on arrival to join the seminary's faculty back in 1951, he found the school with no funds and in low morale. He was tempted to turn his van around and head for relatives' homes in the East, or perhaps reopen negotiations with other schools that had approached him. Or should he in the face of impossible circumstances stand by what he had taken to be God's indication of His will? He decided to stand by. The following decade was a period of great difficulty, even tumultuous conflict. Many times he was tempted to resign, particularly when tempting offers came from other organizations. But says Grounds, "My wife and I had cast our anchor in 2 Corinthians 5:7, 'We walk by faith, not by sight.' My theory of guidance is very simple. Once we have ascertained the will of God, we ought in faith to continue in the direction He has pointed. If we do that, He in the long run—not necessarily in the short haul—will vindicate Himself and grant us whatever verification He may feel is appropriate."

The Lord removes obstacles. The Israelites, walled in time and time again, found that God could part the Red Sea, send hornets to drive out the enemy, put fear and dread into hostile hearts, and tear down the walls of Jericho (Deut. 2:25; 7:12-26; Josh. 2:9-11; 6:20; 24:12-13).

The faithful women who wanted to anoint Jesus' body started out that first Easter morning in faith, not knowing how that stone, sealed by Roman authority and too heavy for them to move, would be rolled away.

Many students have stepped into a college registration line, without enough money for the next semester, but with some degree of faith, to find on nervously reaching their turn at the cashier's window that a scholarship has been awarded, or funds have been deposited anonymously, making another term financially possible.

Believe God is guiding you. The Psalmist said, "Commit thy way unto the Lord; trust also in Him; and He shall bring it to pass" (Ps. 37:5). Following God's will as best we know, we should believe Christ is working in us to do His will (Phil. 2:13).

The complete knowledge of God's will for our lives is a secret that belongs to the Lord (Deut. 29:29). But though we cannot know everything, we can know something. Faith will help balance these extremes, keeping us from over-concern about the future, yet giving us confidence.

Beverly Shea says, "Dream big. God has a way of honoring people who dream of serving Him in a task bigger than they can handle alone. Have faith that God's plan is at work this minute in your life."

Peace

When we find God's will we will develop a certain inward sense of rest and rightness. Confidence will blossom into conviction that we made the right choice. We will have peace. But since feelings are so subjective, peace may not be a reliable indicator unless the pertinent signposts have been previously considered.

This principle of peace doesn't mean that we won't have troubles, but that in the midst of turmoil and trial, we will have a quiet, restful delight, confirming that we are doing what God wants. Martyr Jim Elliot wrote in his diary of the sheer joy of doing the will of God.

A young man had to choose between two colleges. Applications to both schools were due the same date. Agonizing over the respective merits of each school, he finally went to bed the night before the deadline, determining to send the application to College A the next day. But he had no peace. After a restless night he awoke to inform his parents that he now thought he had made the wrong decision. But looking at the forms, he discovered the deadline was a week later for both schools, so did more pondering and praying. The lack of peace on College A helped the lad to decide for College B. His decision was followed by confirming quietude.

How does peace operate in guidance? Paul wrote, "Let the peace of God rule in your hearts" (Col. 3:15). The word *rule* means "to decide, arbitrate, umpire," and was used in secular literature to describe decisions made in athletic contests and court actions. We are to let the harmony of soul that comes from the Lord settle with finality matters in which we are trying to discover the divine will. If we have no inner tranquility, but instead confusion, anxiety, distress, and restlessness, we should rethink and repray the whole affair. If quiet of heart, even though his stomach may be full of butterflies, the believer should proceed. A couple near retirement decided to sell their home and move to Arizona. Then they had second thoughts and no peace. After reconsideration they took their home off the market, and peace returned.

Rev. Robert Dugan, who resigned his pastorate to run for Congress in Colorado met a man who had temporarily left the pastorate and was thoroughly troubled. When the other pastor asked Dugan if he felt equally uncomfortable, his reply was a firm and definite No. Dugan said, "I feel perfectly comfortable in my political quest. This seemed to be the Holy Spirit's confirmation that I had made the right decision. Keep in mind that I maintain the determination to remain in the ministry as long as I live—even if elected to Congress. Some people cannot distinguish between the pastorate and the ministry!"

Tremendous satisfaction comes from knowing we are in the center of God's will. The Bible promises that God "wilt keep him in perfect peace, whose mind is stayed on Thee" (Isa. 26:3).

11

Prime Prerequisite

When the Apostle Paul was seeking God's will about visiting the believers at Rome, he utilized practically all the principles we have discussed. (See Romans 1:9-16; 15:20-32.)

His plan to minister at Rome was certainly *biblical*. He possessed a strong, long-time *burden* to see and help them. *Circumstances* played a part. Since his work in Greece was finished, he would visit Rome, but only after personally delivering an offering from the Greeks to the poor saints at Jerusalem. He used *common sense* and logic by planning to visit them on his way to Spain, thus killing two birds with one stone. Getting the offering to the Jerusalem saints was the *duty at hand,* so first things first. He certainly proceeded *step by step*. To Jerusalem, then hopefully to Rome, and then on to Spain.

His *gift* for pioneer missionary work hindered him from-going earlier to Rome where a church had already been planted. His *ability* to bring spiritual blessing fueled his desire to see the Roman believers.

Likely he sought the *advice* of his companions, though the ultimate decision was his. Paul certainly *delayed* quite a while before reaching his decision on going, and *prayed* about it too.

In *faith* he believed that he would not only come to them, but in the fullness of blessing. His arrival at Rome in the will of God would bring joy and *peace*.

Interestingly, though Paul ultimately reached Rome, it was not at the time nor in the way he planned, for he was arrested at Jerusalem, jailed two years at Caesarea, and shipped as a prisoner on his appeal to Caesar's court, showing that God's will is progressive and dynamic.

Paul followed one other principle absolutely essential for anyone wishing to discover the will of God—willingness to do His will. Paul said he was "ready to preach . . . at Rome also" (Rom. 1:15).

Some Do Not Want to Know God's Will

Many Christians do not zealously seek the divine will, lest their heavenly Father says No to a course of action which they strongly want.

Some who profess desire for supernatural guidance have already decided which path they will pursue. A lady was seen tossing a twig into the air three times at a crossroad. "Why did you throw the twig up like that?" asked a bystander.

"To know which way I should go," she answered.

"But why three times?"

"Because it didn't come down the way I wanted to go the first two times."

How human to want deity to rubberstamp our plans, instead of genuinely seeking the divine will. When a priestess refused to let Alexander the Great consult with the oracle at Delphi about the success of his next miliary campaign, he dragged her into the sacred shrine. She, as if submitting, exclaimed, "You are unconquerable, O son." The priestess merely meant that he was unconquerable in getting his way at that moment, but Alexander took it to mean what he wanted to hear—that he would be victorious in his campaign.

James Warwick Montgomery, warning against the elasticity of astrological interpretation, says "that where the answers are ambiguous, people inevitably choose according to self-interest. Thus the floodgates are opened to the reinforcement of evil tendencies rather than the eradicating of these tendencies by the spiritual surgery of the Gospel. The employment of astrology by Hitler and his associates is one of the clearest documented examples of this phenomenon" (*Principalities and Powers*, Bethany Fellowship, Minneapolis, 1973, p. 118).

When people's minds are made up, they dislike receiving correct advice. The leaders of Jeremiah's day did not like to hear the Lord's will, so they lowered him into a pit of mud (Jer. 38:6). A man, told by his doctor to quit smoking, quit all right— his doctor.

A Christian lady, after asking advice of a Christian friend, honestly admitted she knew the Lord's will all along, but was hoping her friend might give her the other answer, thus providing rationalization for her wrong course of action.

Some quipped, "Half of our troubles come from wanting our own way. The other half generally come from being allowed to have our way."

The prime prerequisite for discovering God's leading is willingness to follow that leading. Jesus said, "If any man will do His will, he shall know of the doctrine, whether it be of God, or whether I speak of Myself" (John 7:17). When at the Feast of Tabernacles Jesus' enemies questioned the source of His teachings, He answered that He was schooled in the seminary of His heavenly Father. Moreover, if anyone really wanted to know God's will, he would know whether His teachings came from God or merely expressed His own ideas.

Herein lies the basic principle in ascertaining the will of God. A direct connection exists between the will of God and a willing heart. If anyone wants to know God's will, God will see that he learns the truth. The more willing we are to do His bidding, the more certain the understanding of His will. Direction is God's responsibility. The Head is to lead. The followers are to follow. If followers aren't willing to follow, the Head will not lead. Surrender precedes knowledge. He guides the guidable. When sheep are willing to heed His voice, the Shepherd will enable them to follow Him (John 10:27).

Bible verses on *doing* the will of God far outnumber those on *knowing* the will of God. Once you're committed to do, knowing should easily follow.

George Muller made submission the first step in determining God's will. "I seek at the beginning to get my heart into such a state that it has no will of its own in regard to a given matter. Nine-tenths of the trouble with people is just here. When one is truly in this state, it is usually but a little way to the knowledge of what His will is."

Dr. Wesley A. Olsen, Executive Vice-president of Northeastern Bible College, says, "The method of finding God's will is not nearly as important as the disposition of the heart. Regardless of the method, and sometimes we use 'stupid, mechanical' ones, I do not believe that the Lord will let us make a mistake if we sincerely want His will. He is more eager to show us His will than we are to seek it." F. B. Meyer said that "obedience is the stepping stone to vision."

More than Curiosity

The attitude of many is, "Lord, tell me what Your will is, then I'll decide if I wish to do it." It's a sort of "If I like what I see, I'll accept it." Ralph Davis of the Africa Inland Mission used to say, "If we were as desirous of doing God's will as we are of knowing God's will, we would know it."

God does not show His will to satisfy curiosity. We are to seek God's will, not that we may peruse it, but that we may pursue it. Even curiosity about God's will for someone else was rebuked by Jesus. When Peter asked Jesus how John would die, Jesus told him, in effect, that it was none of his business (John 21:23).

The attitude of wanting to take a peek at God's will before committing oneself to it betrays lack of faith in the goodness of God. It seems to say, "God, I don't trust you. I think You are going to short-change me." Subconsciously we think that the choice is between doing our will and being happy, on the one hand; and doing God's will and being miserable, on the other. This is a travesty of God who, not sparing His own Son, gives us freely with Him all things. Dr. Oswald Hoffman of the Lutheran Hour put it, "Having given us the package, do you think God will deny us the ribbon?" The concept that what I would like to do cannot possibly be the will of God for me should be dispelled from our thinking. The Psalmist said, "Delight thyself also in the Lord; and He shall give thee the desires of thine heart" (Ps. 37:4). It's possible that what you want may be what He wants for you. As is so often quoted, "God always gives His best to those who leave the choice with Him."

Paul Little wrote, "I dislike intensely the phrase, 'surrender to the will of God.' To me, that implies kicking, struggling, screaming. It is like saying, 'There is no other way out. I'm running, but I'm caught. I've got to collapse and surrender. It's all over. I give up.' I far prefer the term, 'affirm the will of God.' If we had any sense at all, every one of us would affirm God's will with confidence and with joy and with deep satisfaction" (*Affirming the Will of God*, InterVarsity, p. 15).

Willingness to Renounce Pet Plans

A girl fell in love with a man her friends advised against marrying. When she became determined to have her way, they asked her to pray about it. With great emotion these words came out, "Thy will—be done—O Lord—but please give me Jimmie!"

Willingness to do God's will means facing the possibility of remaining single. Though marriage may seem the norm, the single life can be equally satisfying and rich. Many men and women have given up the right to marriage to do some pioneer work, discovering that the abundant life is found in the surrendered life, whether single or married. Florence Nightingale, "the angel of Crimea," turned down an offer of marriage in order to follow the profession of nursing, because she believed it was the Lord's will for her.

Quite the opposite was the experience of Mrs. V. R. Edman, which she related at her husband's inauguration as president of Wheaton College back in 1941. As a recent Bible school graduate and working in a Boston rescue mission, she was interested in pioneer missionary work. With no call to any specific field and with no prospect of a life's companion, while walking in the woods in Old Orchard, Maine, she came to a little clearing, kneeled beside an old pine stump, and poured out her heart to God. She affirmed her willingness to do anything He would chose. She said, "I felt the Lord had heard my prayer, and would lead me where he chose. The next day I met my future husband."

Some try to hang on to a job or goal because it's comfortable or certain, when God may be leading in a new direction. There should be no reservation in any area of life including type of vocation or place of labor, even if it involves a lower salary scale, reduced standard of living, farewell to family and friends, and living in an alien culture.

Dr. Nathan Bailey, who has served as president of both the Christian and Missionary Alliance and of the National Association of Evangelicals, as a young pastor received a unanimous call to a prosperous church in the Pacific Northwest. From every standpoint the offer was most attractive. When Bailey drove into the countryside to pray for leading, even the cloud formations seemed to portray the scenic snowcapped Olympic Mountains near the beckoning church. But he received no clear guidance. He began to realize that underlying the entire procedure was his personal desire to accept the call. When he rejected the invitation, peace came immediately. Later events confirmed that in laying aside personal preference he had found God's leading.

We Must Make a Surrender

Believers are exhorted to "present your bodies a living sacrifice, holy, acceptable unto God, which is your reasonable service. And be not conformed to this world: but be ye transformed by the renewing of your mind, that ye may prove what is that good, and acceptable, and perfect, will of God" (Rom. 12:1-2).

There is a condition between personal surrender and knowing God's will. "Don't let the world around you squeeze you into its own mold, but let God remold your minds from within, so that you may prove in practice that the plan of God for you is good" (Rom. 12:2, PH). You will be transformed, and God will reveal His good, acceptable, and perfect will.

In his *Commentary on Romans,* Charles Hodge says that proving the will of God may be either a purpose or a result of that renewal or change of the mind. Either renewal is a state by which we can discover the will of God, or renewal will yield as a result our approval of what is God's will. The knowledge of God's will is the design and the result of this transformation (published in 1846 by W. S Martien, Philadelphia, pp. 288-289).

John Wesley was scheduled to stay several days

with a certain family in England. Two of the sons did not share their father's enthusiasm for this preacher-guest, so one of them, hiding in a chimney in a corner of Wesley's bedroom, called out in the middle of the night in a sepulchral voice, "John Wesley." Awaking, Wesley replied, "Yes, Lord, here am I." The voice continued, "The Lord hath need of thee in Birmingham." Silence followed. Next morning Wesley came down to breakfast with his bag packed. After eating, he left for Birmingham, to the puzzlement of his host and to the uneasy relief of the sons. Fooled though he was, his utter abandonment to what he thought was the will of God was a factor in the divine guidance he so continuously received. God is not going to waste His time issuing orders to a person who is uncertain about carrying them out.

Almost the first question the newly converted Saul asked was, "Lord, what wilt Thou have me to do?" No wonder the Lord showed him His will (Acts 9:6).

The supreme example of willingness to do God's will was Jesus Christ Incarnate, who said, "Lo, I come to do Thy will, O God" (Heb. 10:9). As a 12-year-old in the temple, He said, "I must be about My Father's business" (Luke 3:49). His meat was to do the will of the Father (John 4:34; 5:30; 6:38; 8:29; 17:4). In Gethsemane He prayed, "Not My will, but Thine, be done" (Luke 22:42).

Of the will of God, F. W. Faber wrote,

> Thou wert the end, the blessed rule
> Of Jesus' toils and tears,
> Thou wert the passion of His heart,
> Those three-and-thirty years.

Gospel singer Beverly Shea says the turning point

in his Christian life came in 1936 in New York City when he was 27 and still searching for an area of service in God's will. Though he did some religious singing on the side, he enjoyed his job in the insurance business, and thought that might be God's will for his career. A friend told him about auditions at CBS to be held for the Lynn Murray Singers. A spot with that top singing group paid a salary double his insurance job, and gave national radio exposure.

About 20 singers were auditioned and politely dismissed before Shea's turn. After his number Lynn Murray asked for another, then gave him a number to learn at home. Shea noticed swearing in the text. Praying about the matter, he realized he couldn't sing that piece. Willing to do God's will, he knew he would have to decline the offer. Next day a phone call came, "Congratulations, Mr. Shea, you are now one of the Lynn Murray Singers." But Shea did not accept, even when a second attempt was made to sign him up.

A few months later after singing in a Sunday night service at Pinebrook Bible Conference in the Pennsylvania Poconos, Dr. Will H. Houghton, president of Moody Bible Institute, called him aside. "Ever thought of making Christian radio your vocation?" Though Shea answered No, Houghton told him of an opening at Moody's Chicago station WMBI.

The following Thursday a letter came from Houghton. Before Shea and his wife opened it, they prayed, for a move to Chicago would mean leaving the East and family and friends. The letter contained a firm offer from Moody Bible Institute to be an announcer on the radio station and soloist on

Dr. Houghton's new network program, "Let's Go Back to the Bible." Years later, as Billy Graham's soloist, Shea reflected how his acceptance to sing with the Lynn Murray singers would have precluded the Chicago opportunity. Willingness to do God's will brings knowledge and delight.

Asked to describe in a few words his idea of consecration, a Sunday School teacher replied, "To sign your name to a blank sheet of paper, and let God fill it in as He wills."

At each triennial Urbana Missionary Convention, students are invited to sign World Evangelism Decision Cards, indicating one of two things: either that God is leading them into overseas service, and that they will pray and plan with this objective in mind; or that though not yet sure of God's will, they are ready to go wherever He leads them. In 1970 close to 15 percent signed. In 1973, 38 percent. In 1976 with 17,000 present, about 50 percent.

Paul Little suggested the following prayer, "Lord, You've created me and I belong to You. You loved me enough as a rebel against You to die for me when I couldn't have cared less for You. Everything I am and have belongs to You. I am not my own. I am bought with a price, with the precious blood of Christ. I consciously and joyfully commit myself to You. Do with me what You choose."

In the diary of the founder of the South Africa General Mission was found this motto, "The will of God, nothing less, nothing more."

12

If I Miss God's Will

A high school girl felt a strong call to foreign missionary service. While preparing for overseas service in Bible school, she met a charming lad. He was a Christian but without interest in foreign missions. She dropped all contact with the missionary board to which she had applied, married the boy, and settled down to a happy wedded life but to lukewarm Christian service. Gnawingly deep within, she wonders if she missed God's best for her life.

A young man sensed that God was leading him to be a doctor. After a year of medical school, he took a lucrative summer job to earn some money. He stayed on the job, because he wanted to get married and buy a house. He never did return to medical school. Though successful in his company, and financially prosperous, he has the nagging feeling that he has missed the will of God for his life. Does he need to spend the rest of his life with that disturbing thought always running through his mind?

According to counselors, these are not isolated instances. Many picture the will of God like an egg which, when broken like Humpty Dumpty, can never be put back together again. A common conception seems to be: "If I step out of the will of God, my Christian life is irreparably ruined. Once I'm sidetracked, it's all up. I'm a spiritual failure."

It's Possible to Turn Off
of the Path of God's Will

The pilot of a low-flying plane spotted a black bear cub, with a 20-pound coffee can wedged tightly over its head, walking around in swift, hopeless circles near a main Alaskan highway. The cub had stuck its head in the can while rummaging around a garbage area, and couldn't extricate itself. According to the pilot, the bear had made five or six huge circular paths, walking over a hundred miles at least. A rescue party, flown into the area, shot tranquilizers into the cub, then cut the can off with a pair of tin snips. On his return flight, the pilot saw the same black bear on its feet walking in a straight line.

The bear's experience reminds us of the wanderings of the Israelites. When they fled Egypt, the journey from the Red Sea to Kadesh-barnea, southernmost city of the Promised Land, should normally have taken 11 days (Deut. 1:2). But because of disobedience, they meandered 40 years in the wilderness. At the end of that period the Lord told them they had circled Mt. Seir long enough, ordering them to turn northward (vv. 3-7). It's possible for a believer to spin his wheels, wandering in aimless circles in a spiritual wilderness, never really reaching his spiritual goals.

It's Possible to Get Back into the Will of God

It's not over when we miss the will of God. We should dispossess ourselves of the mistaken notion that, if we deliberately turn away from God's will, we are forever thrown on the ashheap. Satan would muddle our minds into thinking we are beyond salvage, doomed to God's second best. God never discards a repentant life. Restoration qualifies us for renewed service.

One of the most comforting verses in the Bible is Jonah 3:1, "And the word of the Lord came unto Jonah the second time." God's word had come the first time, "Arise, go to Nineveh, that great city, and cry against it" (1:1-2). But Jonah willfully disobeyed. Instead of heading eastward 500 miles to Nineveh, he found a boat going westward 2,000 miles to the end of the known world, Tarshish. So determined was his opposition to the will of God that he declared he would rather be thrown overboard than return. To bring him back, the Lord prepared a great fish which swallowed, preserved, and then ejected him on home territory.

Wouldn't we think that though God had saved the prophet, He would have had enough of Jonah, and that Jonah would now have disqualified himself from ever again serving as a prophet to proclaim a message from God? Wouldn't God be correct if, in accepting Jonah's repentance, He benched him from further usefulness?

But turning our backs on God's will doesn't bar us from subsequent service. God's commission came a second time to Jonah. Obedience this time resulted in one of the greatest mass conversions in all history, the entire population of Nineveh. If, like Jonah, we have messed up our lives by disobeying the call of God and wasting some of our best years in worthless pursuits while running away from God, our lives can be brought out of their nose dives.

Second Chance

Ours is the God of the second chance (in this life). God spoke to Abraham in Ur of the Chaldees, commanding him to get out of Mesopotamia and to go to a Promised Land (see Acts 7). But halfway there, a long distance from Canaan, he settled down in Haran, a city probably quite similar to his background. Perhaps the feebleness of his father, or fear of traveling into an unknown territory, caused Abraham to give only partial obedience. But God's word came a second time, repeating the earlier command to leave country and kindred for "a land that I will show thee" (Gen. 12:1). This time Abraham went all the way to Canaan (v. 5). His full obedience has brought blessing to the nations of the earth through his descendants who gave us the knowledge of God, the Word of God, the church, and the Saviour.

Moses had a second chance. Though raised in Pharaoh's palace and destined for prominence in Egypt, he chose to suffer affliction with his own people. One day he killed an Egyptian, supposing that "his brethren would have understood how that God by his hand would deliver them" (Acts 7:25). This statement implies some knowledge on Moses' part of his call to be the emancipator of his people But his precipitous act forced him to flee to Midian, where he lived on the back side of a desert for the next 40 years. Seemingly, Moses had ended his liberator assignment. Yet when he was 80 years old, God spoke to him from a burning bush, saying, "Come now therefore, and I will send thee unto Pharaoh, that thou mayest bring forth My people . . . out of Egypt" (Ex. 3:10). God gave him another chance. Even when Moses then offered two excuses, lack of credibility and lack of eloquence, the Lord continued to deal graciously with him.

David, who seduced Bathsheba and had Uriah killed in battle, indicated in his psalm of repentance that not only would the joy of salvation be restored to him, but also that a renewed commission would enable him to teach transgressors the divine way (51:10, 13).

Peter needed another chance after so shamefully denying his Master three times, especially after boasting he would die before he would deny. How often Peter must have wept bitterly in those interim hours between his denial and the resurrection day when Jesus interviewed him privately. Later by the Sea of Galilee, the Lord publicly commissioned Peter, "Feed my sheep." What a power Peter became!

Not only does God give us a second chance to do His bidding, but He gives a third, and a fourth. Surely He Who spoke of forgiving 70 times seven could be called the God of the 490th chance.

Do God's Will From Now On

A college halfback made a costly blunder in the first half of a game, resulting in a touchdown for the opposition. At halftime he sat dejectedly in a corner. When the coach announced that the same players would start the second half, he didn't move, but mumbled something about ruining the game and letting his team down. The coach, placing his hands on the player's shoulder, said firmly, "The game is only half over. Get up and go out there!" That player played an inspired second half.

If we have missed God's will at some point even if for years, we shouldn't panic or despair. Rather we should ask His forgiveness, and then hear Him say, "The game is just part over. Do My will from now on!" We should pick ourselves up, and wherever we are, do His bidding from there on in.

What He has for us from that point on may not be what He first called us to. Let's go back to that student mentioned in the second paragraph of this chapter who dropped out of medical school so he could marry and set up a nice home. Through the years the Spirit kept dealing with him, but without response. A tragedy involving his little girl brought him to the place of surrender. Though it was then too late for him to go back to medical school, he joined the local ambulance corps, as well as devoting several hours a week to tutoring high schoolers who needed help in chemistry.

All is not lost if we have turned from God's best. By doing God's will from here on in, what we think is "second-best" service can be used by the Lord to a first-rate degree.

Some use their former disobedience as a cop-out to do nothing. Others are genuinely paralyzed into inactivity. But we shouldn't quit. The highest, first, and best will of God is that duty right at hand. He can use a clean vessel today. Whatever would now please God the most, regardless of previous mistakes, is God's best for me.

Jonah, Abraham, Moses, David, and Peter all

went on to do God's bidding after disobedience. Also John Mark, a missionary helper who ran away from hardship in Asia Minor, found that his defection did not disqualify him from later missionary service. The gracious Barnabas gave him a second chance. Later, even Paul, who had refused him another chance, found him profitable for the ministry (2 Tim. 4:11). Mark wrote the second book in the New Testament.

The Matter of Consequences

Though it is possible to step back on to God's path after years of disobedience, we may have to suffer certain consequences. Jonah discovered that, in the divine geometry, a detour is the roughest distance between two points.

When the Israelites, tired of manna, lusted after the food of Egypt, the Lord sent them quail. But along with granting their request, He "sent leanness into their soul" (Num. 11:4-6; 31-33; Ps. 106:15).

A girl wandering from God's will took an overdose of drugs. Though today she serves in various capacities in her home church, she is unable to go to the mission field as she had planned because of permanent physical damage.

Another girl married an unbeliever, resulting in continuous, nagging, marital conflict that kept her from her desire to do regular active Christian service in her Sunday School, forcing her to settle for helping in a small, weekly ladies' home Bible study. Though we may get back into the place of God's will, sometimes there may be scars.

On the other hand, as we resume God's path, God is able to overrule our mistakes for His glory, making the wrath of men to praise Him. A Christian out of God's will found himself in jail. There God dealt with him. After his release he began a ministry to prisoners, using expertise he would not have had, if he had not spent time behind bars. By His gracious sovereignty the Divine Weaver has a marvelous way of refashioning the tangled, messed-up strands of our lives into a beautiful pattern. This compensatory goodness is expressed in the promise, "I will restore to you the years that the locust hath eaten" (Joel 2:25).

Also, we may profit from a previous mistake. When the word of the Lord came to Jonah the second time, he had learned his lesson, and obeyed. Making an error may help us not repeat it.

Incidentally, no one should be made to feel guilty for failing to enter the ministry or mission field. The job of farmer, truck driver, mechanic, lawyer, or any other honorable occupation is not one iota inferior to so-called full-time Christian service. In fact, for a person to become a preacher, when he has been divinely called to another vocation, is to settle for God's second best.

How futile to keep looking back to what might have been, debating whether we followed the will of God or spurned it, wondering if we did right or not. So often Satan tries to dissuade a middle-aged person or senior citizen from again seeking God's will by suggesting, "You've wasted most of your life. What's the use of starting anew now?" But let's remember that in Jesus' parable the servants, who labored only a brief time late in the day, received the same pay as those who did the master's will from the start of the day (Matt. 20:1-16).

The person who has the slightest urge to get back on God's track, even though off it for years, can believe that God will give a new start. There is a land of beginning again. The Lord invited His Old Testament people, "Ask for the old paths, where is the good way, and walk therein, and ye shall find rest for your souls" (Jer. 6:16).

To a New Testament church which had lost its first love came this advice, "Remember therefore from whence thou art fallen, and repent, and do the first works" (Rev. 2:5).

The importance of the Lord's will is shown by its inclusion in the Lord's Prayer. In the model prayer, Jesus taught His followers to request, "Thy will be done in earth, as it is in heaven" (Matt. 6:10).

How wonderful to be able to say with the psalmist, "He leadeth me."